OSPREY AIRCRAFT OF TH

Mosquito Aces of World War 2

SERIES EDITOR: TONY HOLMES

OSPREY AIRCRAFT OF THE ACES • 69

Mosquito Aces of World War 2

Andrew Thomas

OSPREY
PUBLISHING

Front Cover

At 1740 hrs on the evening of 25 November 1944, Mosquito XXX MM767/RA-D of No 410 Sqn RCAF took off from its base at B 51 Lille/Vendeville, in northern France, for a nightfighter patrol over Germany. At the controls was American pilot Lt A A Harrington, who was on loan to the RCAF. Sat alongside him was his RAF navigator, Flg Off D G Tongue. The crew had previously flown the aircraft on the night of 29 October, when they had succeeded in shooting down an Fw 190 near Venlo, in Holland, to give Harrington his fourth confirmed victory.

The patrol was uneventful for the first hour, during which time the crew was controlled by a mobile radar unit whose call-sign was 'Bricktile'. When the crew switched to a second control unit things started to happen, as Archie Harrington later recalled;

'I was finally handed over to "Rejoice" on vector 130 degrees and told of trade ahead at between 10,000 and 15,000 ft. He told us of "joy to port, 15 miles" and to "steer 100 degrees". The contact was obtained crossing to starboard, 15 degrees above us, and at a range of four miles. We closed fairly rapidly to two miles, then the target commenced moderate evasive action. Visual was obtained at 4500 ft, height 16,000 ft. I closed right in and finally identified the contact as a Ju 88 nightfighter with a Ju 188 tail. It had a Ju 88G-1 blister under the nose, black crosses clearly seen on the wings and radar aerials clearly seen projecting from the nose.

'I dropped back approximately 600 ft and opened fire. Strikes were seen in the cockpit, engines and wing roots, followed by an explosion and debris. The enemy aircraft dived very steeply, and I followed him on AI (Air Intercept radar) and visually. The enemy aircraft was seen to strike the ground and burn. Our Mosquito had been hit by debris as we fired, shaking the aircraft badly. "Canary" plotted the location of the crash site for the enemy aircraft on the ground and this was was given by "Rejoice" as near Muntz, time 2008 hrs.'

The crew had downed Ju 88G-1 Wk-Nr 712295 of 4./NJG 4, flown by ex-bomber pilot Hauptmann Erwin Strobel, who, along with his radar operator Unteroffizier Horst Scheitzke and gunner Unteroffizier Otto Palme, managed to bale out of the stricken aircraft before it crashed near Gelsenkirchen. This was Harrington's fifth victory, thus making him an ace.

Almost immediately Tongue obtained a head-on contact, although the target evaded and appeared to be trying to intercept them. This duel in the darkness went on for about ten minutes before they closed on the tail of Leutnant Fensch's Ju 88G from 5./NJG 4 and shot it down too. Harrington and Tongue then intercepted a third Ju 88G and scored hits around the cockpit, engines and wing roots. Unteroffizier Goebel's aircraft also fell away and crashed. The No 410 Sqn records succinctly summarised the events thus, 'Take off 1740 hrs, landed 2115 hrs. Three contacts, three visual, three combats, three Ju 88s destroyed!'

In an incredible 18-minute period, Harrington was credited with three aircraft destroyed, taking his final score to seven. This made him the leading USAAF nightfighter pilot of the war. This specially commissioned painting by Mark Postlethwaite shows Harrington's Mosquito sending the first Ju 88G diving away to its destruction

---

First published in Great Britain in 2005 by Osprey Publishing
Midland House, West Way, Botley, Oxford, OX2 0PH, UK
443 Park Avenue South, New York, NY 10016, USA

© 2005 Osprey Publishing Limited

All rights reserved. Apart from any fair dealing for the purpose of private study, research, criticism or review, as permitted under the Copyright, Design and Patents Act 1988, no part of this publication may be reproduced, stored in a retrieval system, or transmitted in any form or by any means, electronic, electrical, chemical, mechanical, optical, photocopying, recording or otherwise without prior written permission. All enquiries should be addressed to the publisher.

CIP Data for this publication is available from the British Library
ISBN-13: 978-1-84176-878-6

Page design by Tony Truscott
Cover Artwork by Mark Postlethwaite
Aircraft Profiles by Chris Davey
Index by Alan Thatcher
Origination by PPS-Grasmere, Leeds, UK
Printed in China through Bookbuilders
Typeset in Adobe Garamond and Univers

08 09 10 11 12 13 12 11 10 9 8 7 6 5 4

ACKNOWLEDGEMENTS

The author wishes to record his gratitude to the following former Mosquito pilots and navigators who have given of their time in answering queries and presenting accounts of their actions for inclusion within this volume: Wg Cdr A D McN Boyd DSO DFC, Wg Cdr B A Burbridge DSO DFC, the late AVM E D Crew CB DSO DFC, Wg Cdr W F Gibb DSO DFC, Sqn Ldr D H Greaves DFC, Gp Capt R C Haine OBE DFC, Wg Cdr G H Melville-Jackson DFC, Peter Rudd DFC AE, Gp Capt R D Schultz DFC CD, Flt Lt J C Surman DFC, the late Flt Lt W H Miller DFC and Flt Lt V A Williams DFC

FOR A CATALOGUE OF ALL BOOKS PUBLISHED BY OSPREY PLEASE CONTACT:

NORTH AMERICA Osprey Direct, C/o Random House Distribution Center, 400 Hahn road, Westminster, MD 21157. E-mail: info@ospreydirect.com

ALL OTHER REGIONS Osprey Direct UK, P.O. Bo 140, Wellingborough, Northants, NN8 2FA, UK. E-mail: info@ospreydirect.co.uk

www.ospreypublishing.com

CONTENTS

CHAPTER ONE
PROLOGUE 6

CHAPTER TWO
DEFENDING THE HOMELAND 9

CHAPTER THREE
D-DAY AND AFTER 26

CHAPTER FOUR
NEMESIS OF THE *NACHTJAGD* 59

CHAPTER FIVE
OVER MOUNTAINS AND JUNGLE 76

CHAPTER SIX
EPILOGUE 86

APPENDICES 88
COLOUR PLATES COMMENTARY 92
INDEX 96

CHAPTER ONE

PROLOGUE

De Havilland's Mosquito, whose all-wooden construction gave it the press-inspired nickname of 'the Wooden Wonder', was probably the finest nightfighter to see action in World War 2. Fast, heavily armed and fitted with increasingly sophisticated air intercept (AI) radar, the aircraft was backed by a well-developed air defence radar system and flown by well trained crews. These all combined to make the Mosquito a formidable enemy. Proof of this came in the fact that the most successful Allied nightfighter pilot of the war claimed all 21 of his victories with the Mosquito, and no fewer than 62 other pilots scored five or more kills to become aces. A further 47 aces achieved at least some of their totals flying the aircraft.

The first operational unit to receive the Mosquito was No 1 Photographic Reconnaissance Unit at Benson (see *Osprey Combat Aircraft 13 – Mosquito Photo-Reconnaissance Units of World War 2* for further details). Amongst its pilots at the time was 25-year-old ex-Etonion Sqn Ldr Rupert Clerke, who had gained several victories flying Hurricanes with No 79 Sqn during the Battle of Britain. On 17 September 1941, in W4055, he flew the Mosquito's first operational sortie – a lengthy reconnaissance of the French west coast.

Three months later, on 13 December, No 157 Sqn was formed to introduce the Mosquito NF II nightfighter into service. Based at Castle Camps and led by Wg Cdr Gordon Slade, the unit's first aircraft (W4073, fitted with dual controls) arrived on 17 January 1942. Deliveries were slow, and with only 20 Mosquitoes delivered by April – some of which lacked AI radar – only seven crews had been fully trained in five months. Those that had managed to complete their conversion onto the NF II found that the matt black paint applied to the aircraft reduced its speed by around 20 mph! The one pilot in No 157 Sqn at this time with considerable Mosquito experience was Rupert Clerke, who had been posted in as a flight commander.

Meanwhile, at Wittering, Defiant II-equipped No 151 Sqn, under the command of six-victory Hurricane ace Sqn Ldr I S 'Black' Smith, received its first aircraft when NF II DD608 arrived on 6 April. Once again deliveries were also slow, but gradually 'A' Flight converted. Eight days after the first Mosquito arrived at Wittering, New Zealander Smith was promoted to wing commander. On 26 April, with three pilots operational, 'A' Flight began standing patrols – the squadron's first with the Mosquito.

Earlier that same month the Luftwaffe had begun the so-called *Baedeker* raids on cathedral cities across Britain. The latest in these attacks occurred on the night of 27 April against Norwich, and although No 157 flew their first sorties that night in defence of the city, none of its three AI-equipped aircraft succeeded in intercepting any German bombers. Aside from malfunctioning radars, the crews also had to cope with several other minor problems, including the engine exhausts burning through their cowling covers.

No 151 Sqn at Wittering was the second Mosquito squadron to receive the de Havilland nightfighter, being commanded at the time by Wg Cdr I S 'Blackie' Smith. On the night of 24 June 1942 he finally broke the Mosquito's duck when, in a short space of time, he shot down a Do 217 and an He 111 to claim his final victories. He later commanded No 487 Sqn and took part in the famous Amiens prison raid in February 1944 (*author's collection*)

In July 1942 No 23 Sqn began intruder operations with the Mosquito NF II (Special). One was DD712/YP-R, which was painted in overall sooty-black. This scheme was found to reduce the aircraft's top speed by a full 20 mph. Seen here on 16 September, it flew its first intruder in the hands of Wg Cdr Hoare a week later, but was lost with its crew of Flt Lt Williamson and Plt Off Lavers on an intruder on 29 November (*Michael Bowyer*)

The following night York was raided, giving No 151 Sqn the opportunity to fly its first operational Mosquito sortie. A No 157 Sqn crew also chased a Do 217, although the latter successfully evaded its pursuer. Further patrols were mounted during raids on Norwich and Ipswich on the 29th, but again without success.

Meanwhile, further west at Colerne, 'B' Flight of No 264 Sqn began its conversion from Defiant IIs onto the new fighter on 3 May. Later that month the Mosquito NF II finally drew blood when, in the early hours of the 29th during a raid on Grimsby, Flt Lt Pennington of No 151 Sqn damaged a He 111 over the North Sea, although his aircraft was hit by return fire and he had to fly back to base on one engine. A Do 217 from KG 2 was also damaged by Plt Off Wain, and Sqn Ldr 'Jumbo' Ashfield of No 157 Sqn (in W4099) attacked another Do 217 off Dover but could only claim it as probably destroyed. The Mosquito's first victory was, frustratingly, still awaited.

A week after No 264 Sqn began operations in mid June 1942, success finally came in spectacular fashion on the night of the 24th when No 151 Sqn intercepted a raid on Nuneaton. At 2330 hrs 'Blackie' Smith and his navigator, Flt Lt Kerr Sheppard (in W4097), fired at an He 111 at 8000 ft – they could only claim it as a probable. However, the squadron's operations book soberly recorded the subsequent events;

'Wg Cdr Smith was then vectored onto another He 111 carrying two torpedoes. He sighted it at two miles just moments before a blip was obtained. The Mosquito was at 7000 ft and the enemy aircraft at 8000 ft, and Wg Cdr Smith closed to 300 yards and was about to fire when the enemy aircraft dived vertically. He quickly shot off a one second burst, and strikes were seen on the undersurfaces of the wings and fuselage. The enemy aircraft went down with its port wing burning outboard of the engine and struck the water and continued to burn. This is claimed as destroyed.

'The Mosquito was then vectored onto another enemy aircraft and AI contact followed. This was lost at maximum range, but with further help another one was obtained and followed up, and a visual resulted at 7000 ft. Closing to 300 yards, it was identified as a Do 217, and the remainder of the cannon ammunition was fired into it in one burst, which set the machine, except the wingtips, on fire and part of the engines fell away. Return fire was experienced from two dorsal machine guns, but Wg Cdr

Smith closed to 100 yards and replied with several short bursts of machine gun fire, silencing the enemy aircraft.

'The Mosquito was now smothered in oil and the pilot broke away to attack again, but the enemy aircraft was losing height rapidly at a very slow forward speed and an attack was found to be impossible as the windscreen was covered in oil. The Mosquito then drew alongside and the enemy aircraft flew into cloud, burning fiercely, illuminating the cloud. This is claimed as destroyed.'

Having well and truly broken the Mosquito's 'duck', the pair landed back at Wittering just before 0100 hrs. The squadron claimed several further victories before the month was out, and still more German bombers during July.

That month, No 264 Sqn also became operational, flying 15 sorties. During the last of them, soon after 0100 hrs on the 31st, Sqn Ldr Charles Cooke, who had four successes flying Spitfires, shot down Ju 88A-4 Wk-Nr 2124/M2+AK of 2./KuFlGr 106 near Malvern. His first burst hit the bomber's port engine, which caught fire and broke off before it crashed, but Cooke's words clearly illustrated the difficulty of accurate identification at night;

'I saw two sets of white exhausts and a faint blurred shape about 900 ft above and slightly to starboard against a dark sky. For the next five minutes I kept it in sight whilst we tried to identify it. I finally decided it was a Do 217 and closed to 140 yards dead astern. It had been weaving continuously since the contact was first obtained, and the aircraft did a 90-degree turn to port, whereupon I fired three short cannon bursts in quick succession. Immediately, it burst into a huge sheet of flame (which almost blinded me) and began to spiral earthwards, disintegrating. We both saw it hit the ground, where the incendiaries were seen in the explosions.'

Charles Cooke's first NF II victory thus made him the first nightfighter pilot to become an ace whilst flying the Mosquito. That same night, near Orleans, during an intruder sortie at about the same time, No 23 Sqn's CO, Wg Cdr 'Bertie' Hoare, also claimed his fifth. The Mosquito had created its first aces.

The first pilots to become aces whilst flying the Mosquito did so on the same night – 31 July 1942 – and within minutes of each other! Flying near Malvern, Sqn Ldr Charles Cooke, whose previous victories had been on Spitfires, shot down a Ju 88 for his fifth kill. Almost two years passed before he claimed his next victory – an Fw 190 shot down over France (*WW2 images.com*)

Flying near Orleans on an intruder on 30/31 July 1942, No 23 Sqn's ebullient CO Wg Cdr Sammy Hoare shot down an unidentified aircraft for his second Mosquito victory – and his fifth overall. He later returned to operations in command of No 605 Sqn (*No 23 Sqn Records*)

DEFENDING THE HOMELAND

The recent heavy losses and lengthy summer nights led to a marked drop in Luftwaffe activity over Britain in August, when only one victory was claimed by a Mosquito. It was a significant one, however, as on the night of 22nd/23rd No 157 Sqn at last claimed its first confirmed kill when the CO, Wg Cdr Slade, shot down 6./KG 2's Do 217E Wk-Nr 1152/U5+LP, flown by Oberleutnant Walter Wolff.

A week earlier another unit had begun re-equipping when No 85 Sqn, under the command of seven-victory Havoc ace Wg Cdr Gordon Raphael, received its first T III trainer. The unit's first NF II (DD718) arrived on 15 August, but more significantly, that day also saw 21-year old Flg Off Branse Burbridge perform his first Mosquito flight – he would later become its leading exponent. Burbridge made his first flight in a NF II on 17 September when he conducted a solo hop in VY-H, after which he performed some familiarisation sorties with his navigator, Sgt Webster. The pair flew GCI practice missions for the rest of the month.

On 30 September the first operational Mosquito pilot was elevated to 'acedom' when the newly promoted Wg Cdr Rupert Clerke, who remained briefly with No 157 Sqn, attacked and shot down Ju 88 Wk-Nr 144181/3E+AH of I./KG 6 off the coast of Holland in very poor weather. The Mosquito's first success in daylight was Clerke's fifth, and he later recalled this significant event;

'I sighted an enemy aircraft approaching us from the north-northwest on top of a cloud layer at

One of No 157 Sqn's first Mosquito NF IIs was W4087/RS-B, which is seen here wearing the early sooty black scheme that adversely affected performance. Used both in the frontline and later as a trials aircraft, W4087 survived the war and was struck off charge in January 1946 (*via Norman Franks*)

Wg Cdr Rupert Clerke flew the Mosquito's first ever operational sortie, and later joined No 157 Sqn. On 30 September 1942, off the coast of Holland, he claimed the Mosquito's first daylight victory when he shot down a Ju 88 from I./KG 6. This success also made him an ace (*WW2images.com*)

about 3000 ft. I approached fairly close to identify the contact, but he took no evasive action – he either did not see me or thought I was friendly. I identified him as a Ju 88 and turned onto his tail at about 1500 yards, at which point he apparently opened his throttles in a shallow climb, leaving the cloud layer behind. I was able to overtake him, and when about 1000 yards behind he rammed his nose hard down into a nearly vertical dive, so I opened fire with a short burst of cannon. He then proceeded to go through a series of the most violent diving manoeuvres imaginable, which I was quite unable to follow, so I continued to give him minimum deflection bursts at ranges of 800 to 1000 yards – my observer saw strikes on the starboard wing root.

'I lost sight of him below me, but my observer said that it was going in. When I next saw it, it appeared to be doing a flat spin and two white plumes were coming from the starboard wing, inboard and outboard of the engine. I watched it spinning almost to the sea when I lost sight of it under the wing, but Plt Off Bannister saw the starboard wing break off, complete with engine, just before it struck the sea.'

It was a rare success, and almost three weeks would pass before a Mosquito crew would register the type's next victory. In the early hours of 19 October a force of 30+ enemy aircraft raided East Anglia, and No 85 Sqn was sent up to intercept the Luftwaffe bombers. In the first action experienced by the unit since it had swapped its Havoc IIIs for Mosquito NF IIs, future nine-victory ace Flt Lt Nigel Bunting attacked and damaged a Ju 88, which limped away smoking. Flt Sgt Neil Munro of No 157 Sqn went one better when he succeeded in shooting down a Ju 88

The Australian-manned No 456 Sqn flew Mosquito NF IIs like DD739/RX-X until early 1944, when it converted to NF XVIIs. Having previously served with No 85 Sqn, this particular aircraft failed to return from a bomber support mission to Kassel on 4 December 1943 (*J W Bennett*)

In late 1942 No 264 Sqn sent a detachment of NF IIs to Predannack, in Cornwall, for *Instep* patrols over Biscay. DD636/PS-D, flown by Plt Off Bruce and DD724/PS-G, with Flg Off Pudsey at the controls, are conducting just such a mission in early 1943, when the unit regularly engaged marauding Ju 88s. DD636, having subsequently served with No 307 Sqn, was lost while flying with No 157 Sqn when it suffered and engine failure over Biscay on 19 November 1943. DD724 survived to be scrapped in 1946 (*RAFM*)

from KG 6 off Southwold. He also damaged a Do 217. Munro would subsequently claim No 239 Sqn's first Mosquito kill (a Bf 110) on 28/29 January 1944. One month later, on 26 February, he and his navigator, Flg Off A R Hurley, were killed when their aircraft (NF II DZ247) crashed near Tittlesham, in Norfolk, at the end of a sortie.

The final Mosquito kill for 1942 came on 31 October when Flt Lt Cave of No 157 Sqn shot down a Ju 88D reconnaissance aircraft off Beachy Head during a daylight convoy patrol.

Although there was little in the way of actual combat to keep Mosquito fighter crews busy, Fighter Command pressed on with its squadron conversion thanks to increased deliveries of NF IIs allowing Beaufighter-equipped units to switch to the more potent de Havilland twin. The first to swap types, in October, were No 25 Sqn at Church Fenton and No 410 Sqn RCAF at Acklington. The former flew its first patrols on 14 November, with the Canadians following in December.

That month the Polish-manned No 307 Sqn and the RAAF's No 456 Sqn also began re-equipping at Exeter and Valley respectively.

December also saw small numbers of No 264 Sqn's Mosquitoes detached to Predannack, in Cornwall, for *Ranger* and *Instep* patrols over the Bay of Biscay to counter the threat of Luftwaffe long-range fighters opposing RAF anti-submarine patrols. These became the precursor of regular sorties as the battle over Biscay reached a new ferocity during 1943.

January opened quietly, with No 307 Sqn commencing operations on the night of the 14th when Sqn Ldr Gerard Ranoszek (who had three Beaufighter victories to his name) flew an uneventful patrol. Enemy raids continued over the next few nights, however, and the Mosquito's first kill of 1943 came 48 hours later when Do 217E U5+KR of 7./KG 2, flown by Leutnant Gunther Wolff, was shot down by No 151 Sqn's Flt Sgt E A 'Tex' Knight and Sgt W L Roberts whilst attempting to bomb Lincoln – the entire crew perished. Canadian Knight would claim a second kill (Bf 110) on 20/21 February 1944, but both he and his navigator, Flg Off D P Doyle, were subsequently killed in NF II DZ270 four nights later when it crashed into the Channel.

Soon after Knight got his kill over Lincoln, No 85 Sqn claimed the first of its many victories with the Mosquito. Appropriately, it was the CO, Wg Cdr Gordon Raphael (who was the only pilot to 'make ace' flying the Havoc), flying with navigator Wt Off Nat Addison, who shot down a pathfinder Ju 88 of I./KG 6. A few days later he handed over command to night-fighting legend Wg Cdr John Cunningham, who arrived with his long-time navigator, Plt Off Jimmy Rawnsley.

No 410 Sqn also had cause to celebrate on 22 January, its diary not-

Probably the RAF's most famous nightfighter pilot, Wg Cdr John Cunningham (right) and his navigator, Flt Lt Jimmy Rawnsley (left), arrived on No 85 Sqn in January 1943, and over the next year claimed four victories to take Cunningham's total to 20 (*via C F Shores*)

ing, 'A RED LETTER DAY in the history of No 410 Sqn. We got our first Jerry! There was much rejoicing and everybody has been busily pounding everybody else's back!' Flt Sgt Haight and Sgt Kipling had sent a Do 217 crashing into the sea near Hartlepool.

Some of the squadron's future stars were also flying regularly, notably Sgt Raine Schultz and his navigator Plt Off Vern Williams, building up experience on the NF II. On 1 February it was the turn of Flg Off D J 'Blackie' Williams (in HJ926) to fly his first operational flight when he searched for two enemy 'weathermen'. Later in the month No 410 Sqn moved to Colby Grange for *Ranger* operations, replacing fellow RCAF unit No 409 Sqn.

Enemy raids continued in early March, and on the night of the 3rd 40 aircraft attacked London without suffering any losses to NF IIs from Nos 85 and 157 Sqns. No 410 Sqn had more luck over East Anglia, however, when on the night of the 18th 'Blackie' Williams, with Plt Off Dalton, in HJ936 downed Do 217E Wk-Nr 5523/U5+AH of 1./KG 2. The aircraft, flown by Unteroffizier Horst Toifell, did not go down without a fight, Williams noting in his combat report that, 'I obtained visual contact with a Do 217 which attempted to dive out. I followed him down and pulled out at 1800 ft. We saw crimson fire, leading us to believe that it had crashed'. The squadron duly claimed one destroyed, but an anti-aircraft battery also claimed it, so Williams was credited with a half share.

Further west, patrols continued over Biscay, and on 22 March No 264 Sqn claimed the first Mosquito *Instep* victory when its crews shot down two Ju 88Cs of 14./KG 40 – Wk-Nr 360052/F8+BY, flown by Leutnant Artur Theis, and Unteroffizier Werner Steurich's Wk-Nr 360352/F8+HY. One of the successful pilots was future ace Flt Lt Walter Gibb, flying DD727, who shared the destruction of a Ju 88 with Flg Off Muir, while the other fell exclusively to Wt Off McKenzie.

During March Wg Cdr Cunningham's No 85 Sqn formed 'C' Flight with three Mosquito NF XVs specially modified for high altitude operational trials aimed at defeating high-flying German bombers. Despite MP469 reaching 44,600 ft on 10 April with Flt Lt Nigel Bunting at the controls, all the NF XVs were eventually withdrawn from use in August after the high altitude threat waned.

Sporadic enemy attacks on Britain continued through to the end of March, with 47 bombers hitting Norwich on the 31st for example.

March also saw No 85 Sqn issued with early production examples of the Mosquito NF XII, which was essentially a NF II fitted with Merlin 21 or 23 engines. The aircraft also boasted four 20 mm cannon and a ten-centimetre AI Mk VIII radar antenna in a 'thimble' nose. The first NF XII victory came on 14/15 April when future ace Sqn Ldr Peter Green, in VY-F, shot down 4./KG 40's Do 217E F8+AM off Clacton for the first of his 14 Mosquito victories. Also successful that night was Flt Lt Geoff Howitt who, with his navigator Flg Off George Irving, shot down

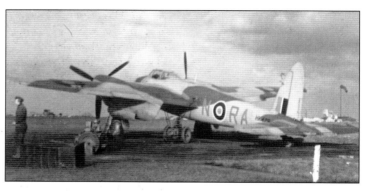

Flg Offs Rayne Schultz and Vern Williams of No 410 Sqn were flying Mosquito NF XIII HK429/RA-N on the night of 13 February 1944 when they sent a Ju 188 crashing into the sea in flames (for their fifth kill), but their aircraft was badly hit by return fire and only just made it back to base. Repaired, the fighter spent time with Nos 604 and 409 Sqns following its spell with No 410 Sqn. Worn out from almost two years of solid frontline flying, HK429 was scrapped in late 1945 (*Canadian Forces*)

Do 217 U5+DP of 6./KG 2. The bomber, flown by Unteroffizier Tannenberger, also crashed into the sea off Clacton to give future six-kill ace Howitt his third victory.

Patrolling in the same area, No 157 Sqn's Flt Lts 'Ben' Benson and Lewis Brandon (in NF II DD730) shot down Unteroffizier Schmurr's Do 217 U5+KP also of 6./KG 2, which crashed into heath land near Colchester. Schmurr and two others baled out, but one of the crew was killed. Benson wrote after the engagement;

'We got AI contact at 10,000 ft on an aircraft dead ahead, crossing from starboard to port. We did a hard turn to port and dived, as the aircraft was 1000 ft below. Visual contact was obtained as we came in behind the aircraft, and we were a little above it as it began weaving gently and changing its height. We climbed and it started losing height. We closed in rapidly and identified the aircraft as a Dornier 217.

'At 200 yards I gave him a three-second burst with four cannon from astern and above, but saw no results. At 150 yards I fired a seven-second burst and saw strikes on the port engine and mainplane, which immediately burst into flames. These spread down the port side of the fuselage until the whole aircraft, including the tail, was ablaze. There was no return fire and it went down in a shallow dive, turning to port, and finally hit the ground.'

Benson's third victory was also the first of eight he would eventually achieve on the Mosquito.

SCHNELL-BOMBERS

With the night defences – increasingly centred on the high performance Mosquito – taking an unacceptable toll of German bombers, the Luftwaffe introduced the single-seat Fw 190A fighter-bombers of SKG 10 to the assault on southern England on 19 April. Initially meeting with little success, the *schnell*-bombers quickly began to make their mark in a series of raids on coastal cities. As a counter to this new threat, Nos 85 and 157 Sqns were moved to West Malling and Hunsdon on 13 May.

As well as having to run the gauntlet of ever increasing defences protecting British cities, the German bomber force also had to contend with a mounting campaign of night intruders attacking their bases in occupied Europe. As this offensive gained momentum, these missions

For offensive work some nightfighter squadrons also used Mosquito FB VIs flown by stand alone *Ranger* flights. One such unit was No 157 Sqn, to which HP850 belonged. The aircraft flew its first operation on 15 August 1943, when Flg Off J L Clifton conducted an intruder that saw him shoot up several locomotives in the Amiens and Juvincourt areas. The aircraft was soon transferred to No 464 Sqn, with whom it was shot down near Metz/Woippy on 3 October 1943 (*F P Bodey*)

were not only flown by specialised units like NF II-equipped No 23 Sqn, but also by nightfighter squadrons. During one such mission to Evreux on the night of the 14/15 May, Flt Lt Herbert Tappin of No 157 Sqn shot down an Fw 190 for the first of his three Mosquito victories with the unit.

The first of these new raiders to fall on English soil was shot down the following night when I./SKG 10's Fw 190s were intercepted by No 85 Sqn's Mosquitoes as they approached the south coast at low level over the Channel. Sqn Ldr Peter Green, with Flt Sgt Grimstone, claimed the first aircraft, which crashed near Dover, while Flt Lt Geoff Howitt got another south of Hastings.

A third Fw 190 fell to future ace Flg Off Bernard Thwaites, with Plt Off Bill Clemo, in VY-L off the French coast. The crew had initially chased another intruder back across the Channel, but prior to opening fire on the aircraft they were recalled by their ground controller, only to then spot their eventual victim as it flew right past them in the opposite direction! Closing to a range of just 50 yards, Thwaites sent the Fw 190 crashing into the sea, although his Mosquito was also damaged by debris from the doomed fighter-bomber. Thwaites then fired on another aircraft and was able to claim it as a 'probable', although this appears to have been upgraded by HQ Fighter Command to a kill. No 85 Sqn also bagged a fifth Fw 190, which fell to Flg Off Shaw.

Although HQ Fighter Command had initially expressed fear that the *schnell*-bomber threat could be difficult to contain, No 85 Sqn had swiftly and dramatically dispelled any concerns during the course of just one engagement. Forty-eight hours later the squadron's promising team of Flg Off John Litott and Sgt George Gilling-Lax shot down yet another Fw 190A (this time from 2./SKG 10), which was one of thirteen despatched to attack targets in southeast England.

No 85 Sqn's almost personal battle with the *schnell*-bombers of SKG 10 continued in the early hours of 22 May when Sqn Ldr Edward Crew, who already had eight victories to his name from previous nightfighter operations in Blenheims and Beaufighters, was scrambled to the southeast by GCI. He told the Author many years later;

'We ended up at about 3000 ft, and with no joy there, we were about to give up the chase when we gained an AI contact well below us and off to our starboard side. Immediately reducing speed and descending, I then

Mosquito NF XII HK119/VY-S of No 85 Sqn lifts off from Hunsdon for an air test during mid-1943. The aircraft was often flown by future ranking Mosquito ace Flg Off Branse Burbridge during the summer and autumn of that year. Prior to its association with Burbridge, HK119 had been used by Flt Lt John Lintott, on the night of 29 May 1943, to claim the third of his four victories when he shot down a Ju 88S of I./KG 66 (*J D R Rawlings*)

spotted the moon reflecting off his canopy! I positioned below and behind and identified the contact as a Focke-Wulf Fw 190 – a tricky opponent. I closed to about 100 yards behind the aircraft and fired a short burst, which immediately caused a large flash, following which the fighter turned as I fired again. This time one of its undercarriage legs fell down. As I was positioning for another attack, the Fw 190 just turned over and went into the sea with a terrific splash. Sadly, there was no sign of the pilot.'

A week later Flg Off John Lintott and Sgt George Gilling-Lax, in HK119/VY-S, shot down the first of the fast Ju 88Ss to fall over England. Patrolling near Lewes, they succeeded in bringing down NL+EX of I./KG 66 after having first climbed to 29,000 ft in order to make contact with their quarry. Lintott's fire apparently hit the bomber's nitrous oxide tanks, which exploded with spectacular force. Sadly, these rising stars were themselves lost on 9 July 1943 when their aircraft crashed at Maidstone soon after they had claimed their fourth victory (Do 217K-1 Wk-Nr 4510/U5+FP, of 6./KG 2, flown by Oberleutnant H Zink, which crashed near Detling). It is believed that this aircraft was heading home after dropping eight bombs on East Grinstead high street. At least one of these scored a direct hit on the Whitehall Cinema, killing 108 civilians and Service personnel and injuring a further 235.

During May still more units replaced their Beaufighters with Mosquito NF XIIs, including Bradwell Bay-based No 29 Sqn, which flew its first sortie (made by Sqn Ldr Arbon in HK164) on the 31st. No 256 Sqn, which had recently moved to Ford, also swapped its Beaufighter VIFs with NF XIIs at this time. The unit flew its first sortie on the night of 21/22 May, when crews participated in two chases, but enjoyed no success.

However, on 11 June the squadron launched eight aircraft on dusk patrols, and Flg Off Cyril Bennett and Sgt Robert Smith shot down a Do 217 at sea level over the Channel 30 miles south of Selsey Bill. This was the squadron's first Mosquito victory, as well as the first of four for this crew. Bennett, who later served as a flight commander with No 515 Sqn, and Smith were subsequently killed when their Mosquito FB VI failed to return from a mission on 13 January 1945.

Biscay battles

The Biscay *Instep* patrols were also continuing to counter the enemy's direct long-range fighter support to transiting U-boats. Amongst others, No 25 Sqn had a detachment of three aircraft at Predannack in support of No 264 Sqn, as well as flying regular intruder missions to the continent. One of the pilots on the detachment was future seven-kill ace Flt Lt Joe Singleton, who, by damaging a Do 217 in January, had made the squadron's first Mosquito claim. During the afternoon of 11 June, while flying DZ685, he led a patrol from both squadrons into Biscay. Here, the crews soon spotted a formation of five Ju 88s from V./KG 40, and Singleton later reported;

'When the enemy aircraft were about 2000 ft above us, I ordered the section, which was then at 5000 ft, to break and go into the attack. I selected the rearmost in the formation and, doing a climbing turn to port inside it, opened fire with a full deflection shot, giving a short burst of less than one second with cannon. The enemy's port engine emitted considerable volumes of thick black smoke, and he peeled off to starboard in a dive. I followed on his tail and gave him another short burst from dead astern, slightly above, and sheets of flame were seen outboard of his port engine.

'The aircraft pulled out of the dive and I followed, closing in to within 25 yards and giving it another three-second burst from dead astern. Flames appeared outboard of the port engine, followed by black smoke from its starboard engine. I again followed, overtook and from slightly above gave a burst from the starboard quarter. Bits of cowling from the starboard engine and pieces of the Junkers' mainplane flew off, and immediately afterwards two of the crew were seen to bale out as the aircraft turned over and hit the sea in a vertical dive.'

Ju 88C Wk-Nr 360288/F8+HZ of 15./KG 40, flown by Feldwebel Fritz Hiebsch and his crew (all of whom perished), was Joe Singleton's second victory. These patrols were no sinecure, however, as two days later two of No 25 Sqn's aircraft – DZ685 and DZ688 – were lost over Biscay, along with one from No 410 Sqn. The four Mosquitoes had been jumped by a section of Fw 190s from 8./JG 2, and two had fallen to Oberfeldwebel May and the other to Feldwebel Schnoll. Another was lost the next day.

Nonetheless, the Mosquitoes remained in the ascendant, with No 151 Sqn getting two more Ju 88s before the end of the month, while a night attack by No 264 Sqn on Biscarosse seaplane base destroyed four flying boats. One of No 151 Sqn's victims on 19 June was flown by Leutnant Willi Guttermann of 14./KG 40 who, with his crew, survived to be picked up by a fishing boat. Their aircraft was the fifth, and final, victim of Flt Lt Henry Bodien, who thus became the latest pilot to 'make ace' on the Mosquito.

A few nights earlier, on 13-14 June, No 85 Sqn's Wg Cdr John Cunningham and his navigator Flt Lt Jimmy Rawnsley achieved their first claim on the Mosquito when, flying DZ302/VY-R, they attacked Leutnant Ullrich's Fw 190A-5 Wk-Nr 840047/CO+LT of 3./SKG 10 at 23,000 ft. Their well-aimed rounds appear to have hit the fighter's controls, as it bunted upwards, flicked and fell near Borough Green, in Kent, although the badly injured Ulrich survived to become a PoW. Cunningham had fired just 20 rounds.

Other light raids by Fw 190s continued throughout the month, and in the early hours of the 21st three aircraft penetrated as far as London. No 85 Sqn's Flt Lt Bill Maguire and Flg Off D H Jones shot down Fw 190A-5 Wk-Nr 840008/GP+LA of 2./SKG 10 into the Medway estuary, killing its pilot, Leutnant Klauer. Maguire would go on to claim a further five victories in Mosquitoes.

MALTA MOVE

Although the Luftwaffe's bomber force continued to pose a significant threat to the British mainland in the summer of 1943, the RAF managed to spare six Mosquitoes from No 256 Sqn to be sent on detachment to Luqa, Malta, to support the invasion of Sicily on 1 July. Fitted with long-range tanks, they left the following evening, led by Sqn Ldr J W Allan and his navigator, Flg Off H J Davidson.

Operating alongside the remaining crews from No 256 Sqn at Ford was the elite Fighter Interception Unit (FIU), which was the principal outfit for operational trials of new equipment in the nightfighter role. It maintained a small fleet of Mosquitoes with which it mounted defensive patrols to trial the latest equipment or tactics.

Two days after No 256 Sqn's detachment had departed for Malta, the FIU's CO, Wg Cdr 'Rory' Chisholm, who was on standby at Ford with Flg Off N L Bamford, scrambled in Mosquito NF XIII HK166 after a 'bandit' flying north at very low altitude. A highly experienced and accomplished nightfighter ace with seven victories to his credit, Chisholm was ordered by GCI to reduce his height as much as possible. Having descended down to about 200 ft, he briefly spotted the fleeing contact heading across the Channel for France. Despite the pitch black, Chisholm regained contact with the enemy aircraft, as he recounted in his autobiography, *Cover of Darkness*;

'The point of light became two, and at 200 yards became four, and round them appeared the silhouette of a two-engined aircraft made vague by the dazzle from the exhausts.'

There then followed an agonising period as they closed on the French coast, worrying about whether the contact was friendly or not, but eventually Chisholm identified the aircraft as a Ju 88;

'Had I to risk all to complete the case? Or should I weigh up the evidence now and act on it? This was hair splitting – the sooner the job was done the better. I opened fire from about 200 yards, aiming between the telltale exhausts. I saw strikes and drew away to the left. A light came on amidships and there was return fire. Now I knew that this was a Ju 88. I came in astern again, and a second burst produced a small explosion in the fuselage. Suddenly the aircraft slowed down and I found myself overtaking alarmingly. I pulled the stick back and sailed up and over, climbing steeply. As we collected our wits, we realised that there was a pool of fire on the sea. We circled over it twice and went back to land, having at least for that night earned our keep.'

July also saw the Luftwaffe make probing attacks along the east coast of England, provoking a swift response from No 410 Sqn, based south of Lincoln at Coleby Grange. First into action was Canadian Sqn Ldr Arthur Lawrence, who had joined the unit the previous month as a flight commander from No 406 Sqn RCAF. He had claimed four Beaufighter victories with his old squadron, and on 13 July he scrambled in NF II HJ944 under 'Orby' GCI after a Do 217 that had been detected off the mouth of the Humber. Lawrence made short work of the Dornier (believed to have been from KG 2), which he shot down into the sea ten miles off the coast. This was his fifth, and last, kill.

A few weeks prior to this engagement a fast new Luftwaffe bomber in the shape of the Messerschmitt Me 410 had made its first appearance in English skies. And on the same night that Arthur Lawrence reached 'acedom', Flt Lt Nigel Bunting of No 85 Sqn shot down the first Me 410 to fall to a Mosquito. The aircraft had come in over Dover and he tracked it towards the Essex coast until he managed to pick out the glow of its exhausts. Closing to 200 yards, Bunting opened fire in NF XII VY-T from below, critically damaging Me 410A-1 Wk-Nr 0238/U5+KG of V./KG 2. Both Feldwebel F Zwissler and Oberfeldwebel L Raida were killed when their aircraft plunged vertically into the sea off Felixstowe. The first Me 410 to fall over Britain was also Bunting's first step to ace status. His squadronmate, and future ace, Bernard Thwaites got another (Me 410A-1 U5+CJ from *Stab* V./KG 2) two nights later.

While his squadron detachment met with huge success in Malta, No 256 Sqn CO Wg Cdr Geoffrey Park saw his element at Ford also adding to the unit's growing victory tally. Amongst the pilots claiming victories was Flg Off Cyril Bennett, who gained the second of his four kills on the night of 17/18 July when he downed a Fw 190 south of the Isle of Wight. Eleven days later Park himself claimed his first kill when he shot down yet another Me 410 from V./KG 2 off Beachy Head. The victorious pilot later recalled in his combat report that 'the enemy aircraft burst into flames, diving into the sea and burning on the water'.

These night engagements were not always without incident, however, as Park could testify following a memorable mission on 15/16 August. He caught a Do 217M from KG 2 in a steep climb southeast of Selsey Bill, and after a short burst it fell away and the crew baled out. Almost immediately Park downed a second Dornier from the same *kampfgeschwader*, before closing on a third. The last Do 217M proved a difficult nut to crack, and it eventually evaded despite Park hitting it in the belly. However, return fire heavily damaged the Mosquito, which, after hitting the Dornier again, limped back to Ford for a crash-landing.

OFFENSIVE PATROLS

As well as defensive patrols, most nightfighter squadrons also mounted offensive sorties over enemy bases to supplement the efforts of the dedicated intruder squadrons (as are described in Chapter 4). The carriage of the latest radar on these sorties was prohibited, so many units were issued with fighter-bomber Mosquito FB VIs for the task. No 410 Sqn's Plt Off Rayne Schultz and Flg Off Vern Williams flew just such an aircraft (HP849/RA-B) on a 'Flower' to St Dizier, as the latter described to the Author especially for this volume;

'Our first successful combat experience occurred on the night of 15 August 1943. We took off from our base at Coleby Grange, in Lincolnshire, to patrol the St Dizier area in order to provide fighter support to our bomber stream. On completion of our patrol, we set course to return to Coleby Grange after sighting no enemy nightfighters. On route we bombed a railway bridge and damaged three locomotives and several railway cars.

'When approaching the coast of France at an altitude of 6000 ft, we spotted an aircraft. Upon closing to intercept, we identified the bogey as a Do 217. As we approached our firing range, the under turret commenced firing at us. At a range of 400 yards we began return fire and the Dornier immediately took evasive action. The visual contact was lost as it dived underneath our aircraft. We followed his descent with the aid of our radar equipment and a visual contact was regained at a range of 6000 ft. We closed to 150 yards and the Dornier recommenced evasive action by carrying out skidding turns. Rayne opened fire and strikes were observed, resulting in burning pieces dropping off.

'Immediately afterwards its crew of four baled out and their aircraft began a shallow dive in the direction of the coast. Rayne closed and gave a burst from our cannons. The starboard wing and engine fell off the burning Dornier, which exploded upon falling into the sea.'

Do 217M-1 Wk-Nr 40702/U5+EH of 1./KG 2 crashed into the sea of fBeachy Head, providing the Mosquito crew with their first of five victims. Canadian Schultz would eventually finish the war with eight kills to his credit.

A combination of sorties such as these and the countering of small-scale intrusions continued through the summer months. The highly effective nightfighter units, now almost completely equipped with Mosquitoes, exacted a steady toll on the Luftwaffe intruders, and a number of pilots claimed regularly. One was Flt Lt Bernard Thwaites of No 85 Sqn, who, on the night of 8 September, with Plt Off Bill Clemo navigating, took off from West Malling for a patrol off Foreland. They were vectored onto a contact about 15 miles away, and closing in, Thwaites gained a fleeting visual contact that was soon lost.

A few moments later he sighted a Fw 190 carrying long-range tanks. Easing the nose back, Thwaites opened fire from 80 yards dead astern and had the satisfaction of seeing the fuselage and engine burst into flames and fall away in a spin to crash into the sea. With virtually no time to congratulate themselves, the crew was quickly vectored onto another enemy aircraft some eight miles away, and eventually Clemo picked up a contact which turned out to be a violently evading Fw 190. It went into a steady climb, and from astern Thwaites once more eased up his nose and opened fire from 100 yards. Again, the enemy aircraft caught fire, with flames running along the wings and fuselage, before it fell away to the left and crashed into the sea. Not only had Thwaites just become the RAF's latest ace with his brace of Fw 190A-5s from I./SKG 10, but he had also become the first in Fighter Command to claim five on the Mosquito.

Shortly before Thwaites achieved 'acedom', No 85 Sqn had seen another small, but significant, event take place when, on 2 September, Flg Offs Branse Burbridge and Bill Skelton undertook their first trip together in a Mosquito when they flew a night flying air test in VY-J – the start of what was to be the RAF's most successful nightfighting team of the war. They gained their first contact with the Luftwaffe on 17 October, but having just acquired the enemy aircraft visually, a cutting starboard engine caused the crew to lose their quarry.

The summer and early autumn also saw the few remaining Beaufighter units re-equip with Mosquitoes. One of those was No 96 Sqn, commanded by nightfighter ace Wg Cdr Edward Crew, who had been posted in from No 85 Sqn. The unit received its first centimetric AI Mk VII-equipped Mosquito NF XII at Drem on 2 October, No 96 Sqn sharing the base with No 488 Sqn RNZAF, which had been issued with its first NF XIIs the previous month – the Kiwis received their NF XIIIs a few weeks later.

Luftwaffe raiders attacked targets in southeast England on 21 nights in October, with the new Ju 188 also being introduced into the attack at this time. More than 500 sorties were flown against London, with the heaviest raid coming on the night of the 7/8 October. No 85 Sqn's 'A' Flight mounted eight defensive sorties on that night alone. Flight commander Sqn Ldr Bill Maguire, in VY-E, had a lengthy fight with an Me 410 (possibly Wk-Nr 10185/U5+KG of 16./KG 2), the pilot

Flg Off Branse Burbridge of No 85 Sqn, having initially flown Havocs with the unit, later converted to the Mosquito and, between February 1944 and January 1945, was credited with 21 enemy aircraft and three V1 flying bombs destroyed (*B A Burbridge*)

spotting the enemy bomber some 900 ft below him. Diving on the Messerschmitt, he eventually lost it near Hastings after a hectic fight, although another Mosquito crew saw it crash into the sea.

A week later, during the evening of 15 October, Maguire brought down Ju 188E-1 Wk-Nr 260179/3E-FL of 3./KG 6 near Ipswich at 1058 hrs and Ju 188E-1 Wk-Nr 260173/3E+BL of 1./KG 6 off Clacton-on-Sea, in Essex, at 1113 hrs. Flg Off Hugh Thomas began his road to 'acedom' by shooting down a second 1./KG 6 machine (Ju 188E-1 Wk-Nr 260177/ 3E+HH) near Birchington at 1115 hrs.

These losses were just three of 28 Luftwaffe bombers downed by the now very efficient defences during a three-week period of intense operations in October-November 1943.

However, against the fast new raiders such as the Me 410 and the Fw 190, the margin of performance between the Mosquito and its quarry was relatively small. This meant that a combination of skilful flying and effective use of AI radar was essential to achieve success. The new NF XIII proved better equipped to deal with the high-speed threat, and at midnight on 8/9 November, the type enjoyed its first success with No 488 Sqn RNZAF when Flg Off Graham Reed destroyed Me 410A-1 Wk-Nr 10311/U5+HE of 14./KG 2 off Clacton-on-Sea for the first of his three kills.

Force Restructure

On 15 November 1943, with the formation of the 2nd Tactical Air Force (TAF) to support and protect the coming invasion of France, RAF Fighter Command was restructured to better support its ever-widening commitments. One element was tasked with home defence, which was clumsily titled Air Defence of Great Britain (ADGB). Ten squadrons of Mosquito fighters and intruders where assigned to this task, along with numerous Spitfire and Typhoon units, while the remaining squadrons were eventually formed into the 2nd TAF's No 85 Group. This was part of the Allied Expeditionary Air Force which was eventually intended to move to the Continent following the invasion.

However, in the interim little changed as all units continued to defend England, and particularly the vulnerable ports, from attack. The first nightfighter squadron to 'migrate' to the 2nd TAF was No 264 Sqn at Church Fenton in December, followed by No 604 Sqn, which replaced its Beaufighter VIFs with Mosquito NF XII/XIIIs in early 1944. In reality, this change of command for these units was little more than a 'paper exercise' only until after the invasion, as the priority remained the defence of the UK and, increasingly, the invasion ports.

It was No 410 Sqn which, having moved south for short period, had perhaps the outstanding individual combat of late 1943. Central to the action was the crew of Rayne Schultz and Vernon Williams, the latter recalling:

'Our second combat sortie occurred on the clear and moonlit night of 10 December 1943 while we were stationed at Hunsdon, in Hertfordshire. That night the Luftwaffe despatched 56 Do 217 bombers to attack a vital ball-bearing factory located at Chelmsford, northeast of London. We were successful in breaking up their bombing effort by destroying three of their number, and many of the remaining aircraft

No 410 Sqn's Rayne Schultz and Vern Williams demonstrate to an American colleague how they fought their action on the night of 10 December 1943, when, in the space of a few minutes, they brought down three Do 217s (*V Williams*)

dropping their bombs other than on their target.

'Our Mosquito (NF II DZ292) was scrambled at 1800 hrs and ordered to patrol north-to-south midway across the North Sea at 15,000 ft. While on our patrol, GCI gave us a course and height to fly to investigate a bogey six miles dead ahead. I picked up a contact on my radar screen, which indicated that it was to starboard and well below us. After overshooting our target, GCI provided additional interception data, enabling me to direct Rayne on a course and height to obtain a visual contact. After closing to 50 yards we identified it as a Do 217, which then took evasive action. We commenced firing, which resulted in a large flash and explosion on the starboard side. At a height of 1500 ft, the Dornier opened its bomb-bay doors and tried to jettison its load. A long burst from our cannons struck and it hit the sea, burning furiously.

'We were then given orders to climb to 15,000 ft. I soon obtained a contact on my radar screen – we were now in the bomber stream, and I could visually see Dorniers to port and starboard of our "Mossie". We closed in and opened fire from dead astern at 300 yards. At a range of 50 ft, the Dornier blew up and we flew through its debris.

'Meanwhile, I had been holding another contact on my radar screen. I told Rayne to turn to starboard and he obtained a visual, which he identified as another Do 217. It took evasive action and descended to sea level. We were able to retain our visual as the Dornier (Do 217M-1 Wk-Nr 722747/U5+CK of 2./KG 2) steadied up and turned for its home base. This enabled Rayne to fire a short cannon burst, which resulted in the bomber's starboard engine catching fire.

'During this engagement the Dornier's gunner fired a defensive barrage. Our Mosquito was repeatedly hit. One cannon shell smashed our instrument panel, missing Rayne by inches. A second burst from our cannons resulted in the Dornier's port engine being set on fire. With both engines ablaze, it crashed into the water near Clacton-on-Sea. At this point our starboard engine started to splutter and our port engine was on fire. We were able to extinguish the fire and Rayne made an emergency one-engine landing at Bradwell Bay.'

The 'Baby Blitz'

1944 began propitiously when, on the second night of the year, John Cunningham and Jimmy Rawnsley used NF XIII HK374/VY-L (which had engines trial-fitted with nitrous oxide injection to boost the fighter's performance) to destroy a Me 410 off Le Touquet – Cunningham's 20th, and final, confirmed victory. There were sterner tests ahead for the RAF's nightfighters, however, as on the night of 21/22 January, the Luftwaffe's Operation *Steinbock* offensive against London began with 447 sorties. The campaign was soon dubbed the 'Baby Blitz' by the British.

CHAPTER TWO

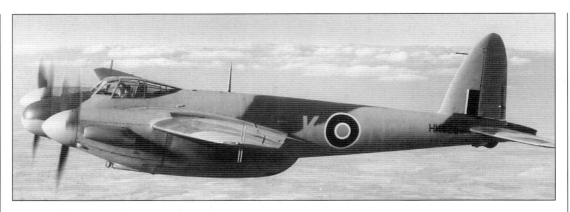

As one of the RAF's longest-serving nightfighter units, No 29 Sqn was equipped with Mosquito NF XIIIs for almost 18 months from October 1943. This particular example (HK428/RO-K) flew its first operation with the unit on 1 May 1944 when Flt Lt King carried out an abortive intercept. Supplied new to the squadron, HK428 subsequently served with the Central Gunnery School prior to being struck off charge in September 1946 (*Official*)

Flt Lt Peter Hall from New Zealand initially flew photo-reconnaissance Spitfires with No 140 Sqn in 1942. Transferred to No 488 Sqn RNZAF in 1943, he duly claimed eight kills and one probable in just nine months flying NF XII/XIIIs. He was one of eight aces to fly with this unit (*WW2images.com*)

In response to this attack, No 29 Sqn scrambled thirteen NF XIIIs, No 85 Sqn four NF XVIIs, No 25 Sqn six NF XVIIs, No 96 Sqn seven NF XIIIs, No 410 Sqn ten NF XIIIs, No 456 Sqn two NF XVIIs and No 488 Sqn eleven NF XIIIs. The NF XII/XIIIs from No 151 Sqn, based at Colerne, were also active. One of its aircraft (NF XII HK193), crewed by New Zealander Wt Off Howard Kemp and Flt Sgt J R Maidment, claimed the first He 177 to be brought down over England when Wk-Nr 5747 of 1./KG 40 hit rising ground as its pilot, Oberleutnant K Waterbeck, tried to force-land the damaged bomber near Hindhead, in Surrey, at 2131 hrs.

This was the crew's second kill, for they had destroyed Ju 88A-14 Wk-Nr 144687/3E+EH of I./KG 6 on 17/18 May 1943. Both Kemp and Maidment were subsequently killed in action during an *Instep* patrol on 11 April 1944 when their Mosquito (MM505) was one of three lost in combat with Ju 88Cs of ZG 1.

Returning to the opening night of the 'Baby Blitz', aside from No 151 Sqn's He 177, six Ju 88s, an Fw 190 and a Do 217 (the latter falling to future eight-kill ace Flt Lt J A S Hall of No 488 Sqn, who also shot down Ju 88A-14 Wk-Nr 550296/B3+AP of 6./KG 54 near Lympne, flying HK380/ME-Y) were downed by the Mosquito crews defending the southeast.

The next big raid came at the end of the month, followed by eight sizeable attacks during February when the extensive use of 'window' (radar-reflecting foil strips) made the nightfighter task more complex. February also saw No 125 'Newfoundland' Sqn, led by nightfighter ace Sqn Ldr Johnny Topham (see *Osprey Aircraft of the Aces 65 – Beaufighter Aces of World War 2* for details), exchange its Beaufighter VIFs for Mosquito NF XVIIs at Valley.

One of the handful of Mosquito pilots to enjoy success during February was Sgt Chris Vlotman of No 488 Sqn, who claimed his first of four kills on the 3rd in NF XIII HK367. Paired up with Sgt J L Wood as his navigator, Vlotman ended the war as the leading Dutch nightfighter pilot.

Around 60 bombers headed for London during the evening of 23 February, and in the early hours Flt Lts Branse Burbridge and Bill Skelton, in VY-Y, were nearing the end of their patrol from West Malling when they had a combat resulting in their first victory. Branse Burbridge recounted the action to the Author especially for this volume;

'After a frustrating sortie, we were over the sea and heading back home when Bill gained an AI contact, so I quickly pulled into a starboard turn and descended and eventually saw a Messerschmitt 410. I managed to get directly behind him and gave a long burst, and as I had not got this close since my Havoc days, I wanted to make sure of it. I need not have worried as its left hand engine promptly burst into flames, which quickly spread, and with a mixture of sadness and elation we saw it explode with considerable violence and go down. After the first hits, Bill and I saw one of the crew bale out and he went just over the top of us. I was glad that someone did get out. That was my first one.'

The most successful Dutch nightfighter pilot was Plt Off Christiaan Vlotman (left), who flew with Sgt John Wood (right) as part of No 488 Sqn. They shot down four enemy aircraft in early 1944 (*E Dowden*)

The Luftwaffe attacks continued with variable intensity and a varying degree of losses through March. On the 14th around 140 enemy aircraft were operating over England, and amongst those who claimed were Sqn Ldr Peter Green from No 410 Sqn (recently transferred to the 2nd TAF), who got a Ju 88, and Lt Archie Harrington, who claimed a Junkers bomber from 2./KG 54.

Harrington, who was a serving officer in the USAAF, had been attached to the Canadian unit to gain nightfighting experience prior to the arrival of the P-61 Black Widow (see *Osprey Combat Aircraft 8 – P-61 Black Widow Units of World War 2* for details) in the UK. Paired up with Flg Off D G Tongue, Harrington enjoyed great success during his time with No 410 Sqn, being credited with seven kills by the end of 1944 – this tally made him the USAAF's leading nightfighter pilot of the war, despite the fact that he never scored a victory in an American aircraft!

Also in action during March was Beaufighter ace Flt Lt Douglas Greaves and his long-term navigator Flg Off Milton Robbins, both of whom had joined No 25 Sqn from a telecommunications flying unit following a successful tour with No 255 Sqn in North Africa. On the 19th they were patrolling off Cromer in NF XVII HK278, as Greaves explained to the Author;

'We took off from Coltishall, vectored to the east and levelled off at 12,000 ft. We immediately obtained a contact crossing from our starboard side about 2000 ft above us. We closed and obtained a visual on a Do 217, and at 50-60 yards I fired a two-second burst from dead astern. It took no evasive action. A further two-second burst caused it to burn furiously, and the bomber dived into the sea, where it continued to burn.

'We were then given another contact 4000 ft above us, and we soon obtained visual contact with a He 177. I closed in to 50-60 yards and gave it a three- to four-second burst from dead astern. Strikes were scored on the fuselage and port motor and it started burning furiously, diving away to port to explode upon hitting the sea.'

Despite grave losses, the Luftwaffe's mission tempo was sustained into April, keeping both ADGB and the 2nd TAF nightfighter units busy.

On 18 April 1944 No 488 Sqn's CO, Wg Cdr Dickie Haine, had just landed at Bradwell Bay when this Ju 88 from 3./KG 54 'appeared' at the Essex base. He promptly arrested the crew, but his claim for 'one Ju 88 captured' was not allowed! (*R C Haine*)

On the 18th No 488 Sqn made another claim, as was recalled to the Author by the unit's CO at the time, Wg Cdr Dickie Haine (who claimed two Mosquito kills later in the year);

'I had just landed from a patrol at Bradwell Bay, and thinking the aircraft slithering down the flare path was one of my Mosquitoes, I leaped into a jeep and arrived in time to see, much to my surprise, German airmen scrambling out of a Ju 88! The ambulance had also just arrived, and I unceremoniously pushed the Germans into the back, along with my navigator, Pete Bowman, and told the driver to take them all to the guardroom! As it drove away, I became a bit concerned about Pete, but all was well in the end. The squadron claimed one Ju 88 captured, but this was never allowed!'

No 488 Sqn's visitor was Ju 88A-4 Wk-Nr 1214/B3+PL of 3./KG 54, which had had its port engine and compass knocked out by flak over London. The crew, led by Unteroffizier H Brandt, thought that they were over Holland, having flown for 90 minutes on one engine searching for the lights of an airfield on which to land. Unfortunately for the four-man crew, the partially lit runway at Bradwell Bay, on the Essex coast, was the first airfield that they spotted.

Recently re-equipped No 125 Sqn, now based at Hurn, near Bournemouth, also began to encounter Luftwaffe bombers in the second half of April. During the evening of the 23rd a sizeable force of bombers from II. and III./KG 30 left France for a raid on Bristol. One of the aircraft sortied was Ju 88A-14 Wk-Nr 144501/4D+FM from 4 *Staffel*, flown by Unteroffizier Rudolf Detering. Shortly after 0100 hrs, No 125 Sqn Mosquito NF XVII HK355/VA-T scrambled from Hurn with Sqn Ldr Eric Barwell at the controls – he was an ace who had claimed his first five victories flying Defiants over Dunkirk in 1940, and survived to tell the tale! Barwell's combat report described the Ju 88's demise;

'A short burst was given from almost dead astern and strikes were seen on the bomber's starboard wing root and engine. The Junkers went down to starboard almost vertically, spinning, with the engine on fire and pieces ablaze falling from the bomber. A glow was seen from the ground where the Ju 88 hit.'

New Ace

Two nights later No 85 Sqn's Branse Burbridge became the RAF's latest nightfighting ace;

'I recall being airborne at over 20,000 ft as dawn was breaking, and being sent off after a contact. Bill (Skelton) managed to get it on our AI, although there was a problem with the radar, so I had to try to keep at the same level as the bandit. I was surprised in the half light as to how difficult it was to see, but eventually I'd got in close enough to see that it was an Me 410. I thus dropped back a little and gave it a very long burst, which resulted in two very bright flashes around an engine, which immediately caught fire. However, spilling oil covered my windscreen and further reduced my view.

'The Messerschmitt was being flown very erratically, and as the cannon in my fighter had probably overheated through continual use, I pulled up alongside the aircraft just as its top hatch opened. I was considering whether to give it another squirt when the Me 410 dived off to port and we followed and watched it go into the sea off Portsmouth.'

Burbridge and Skelton's fifth victim was a photo-reconnaissance configured Me 410B-2 from 1(F)./122, and although its pilot, Oberleutnant H Kroll, was killed, crewman Oberfahnrich W Mayer was fished out of the Solent and made a PoW. Burbridge duly received the DFC for his exploits on 18 May.

The end of the month saw yet another new Mosquito unit introduced to the action when No 406 Sqn RCAF exchanged its Beaufighter VIFs for NF XIIs at Winkleigh, in Devon. On the night of the 29th, flight commander Sqn Ldr D J 'Blackie' Williams, with Flg Off 'Kirk' Kirkpatrick, took off in NF III HU-D on the squadron's first sortie with the new type. In the space of just 11 minutes they claimed the squadron's first Mosquito victories by downing Do 217K-3 Wk-Nr 4701/6N+AD of *Stab* III./KG 400 and Do 217K-3 Wk-Nr 4716/6N+IT of 9./KG 100 – the former crashed into the sea off Plymouth harbour and the later came down in nearby Blackawton. These successes took ex-Bomber Command pilot Williams' total to four, and he would subsequently 'make ace' in July when two more Do 217s fell to his guns.

Two weeks later, on 14/15 May, No 406 Sqn's CO, Wg Cdr R C 'Moose' Fumerton, with Flt Lt Lynes as his navigator, also in HU-D, caught a Ju 88 over the Channel southeast of Portland Bill and sent it down. Fumerton's only Mosquito victory, this took the Canadian ace's tally to 14, and made him the RCAF's most successful nightfighter pilot.

That same night the Luftwaffe raided Bristol and lost 11 bombers. One of these was claimed by the recently re-equipped No 604 Sqn after Flg Off John Surman (in HK527) brought down a Do 217 following a running fight in bright moonlight off the south coast. This was the second of Surman's five victories, the final three coming on the night of 6/7 August.

In spite of the best efforts of the Luftwaffe to disrupt the build up of men and equipment assembling in southern England for the invasion of France, these raids had had little impact on Allied invasion preparations thanks to the combined efforts of anti-aircraft artillery units on the ground and Mosquito nightfighters in the air. On the eve of D-Day six Mosquito nightfighter squadrons formed part of the 2nd TAF, ready to move to the Continent after the Normandy landings. They were Nos 264 and 410 Sqns in No 141 Wing, Nos 488 and 604 Sqns in No 147 Wing and Nos 29 and 409 Sqns in No 148 Wing. The remaining Mosquito nightfighter units remained under ADGB command.

D-DAY AND AFTER

The eve of the great invasion of France saw the Mosquito nightfighter squadrons fully active defending the massive, and potentially vulnerable, landing forces. ADGB had four squadrons with No 11 Group (Nos 96, 125, 219 and 456 Sqns), whilst further west No 10 Group controlled Nos 68 and 151 Sqns, as well as the partially-equipped No 406 Sqn. To the north, No 12 Group had No 25 Sqn and the Poles of No 307 Sqn under its command. ADGB also has operational control of the 2nd TAF's No 85 Group nightfighter units – Nos 29, 264, 409, 410, 488 and 604 Sqns. Other Mosquito fighters were also active on intruder and bomber support duties.

On the night prior to the 6 June 1944 invasion, all the nightfighter squadrons were busy ensuring the safety of the landing force. No 410 Sqn's operational diary for this period was typical for most southern-based Mosquito nightfighter units. From the beginning of June, its crews continued their night patrols over the North Sea, with the groundcrews also working hard to maintain maximum serviceability – typically, 18 of the unit's 22 aircraft were available.

On 5 June No 410 Sqn's CO, Wg Cdr G A Hiltz, led a four-aircraft detachment to Colerne, from where they provided fighter cover to the initial airborne landings later that night. Among the pilots involved was Flt Lt C E 'Pop' Edinger, who was soon to become an ace.

At 0100 hrs on 6 June at the squadron's home base at Hunsdon, the first of four patrols took off, but all proved uneventful – crews all reported that the cloud was layered up to 10,000 ft. A further five patrols were subsequently flown by No 410 Sqn as part of their commitment to the nightfighter 'pool' tasked with covering the 4000 ships of Operation *Neptune* as they crossed the Channel, bound for Normandy.

The unit also sent Flg Off Bill Dexter and his navigator out on a freelance patrol over the Caen area, and they duly became the first members of No 410 Sqn to fly over Normandy itself. The following evening flights patrolled the invasion beaches, although the only contacts they acquired proved to be friendly Lancasters. The squadron flew more patrols over the beachhead on the 7th, and in the early hours of the 8th, as future ace Sqn Ldr Dean Somerville closed on and identified a Lancaster, its rear gunner opened fire. The same thing happened to Lt Archie Harrington, whilst Flt Lt W G Dinsdale was also fired on and his aircraft hit in the wing by yet another Lancaster. Clearly the bomber crews were taking no chances!

No 410 Sqn did not fly on the night of 8/9 June due to very bad weather, although the 2nd TAF nightfighters actually managed to record their first victories since the landings that same night when crews from Nos 29 and 604 Sqns each claimed single kills. Twenty-four hours later, No 410 Sqn bagged its first victim when Flg Off Bob Snowdon and Flt Sgt A McLeod (in NF XIII HK466/RA-J) shot down a Ju 188.

Patrols over the invasion area the next night were under mobile GCI control, allowing many contacts to be investigated. On the night of the

10th, No 264 Sqn claimed its 100th victory of the war, and two nights later Wt Off Walter Price of No 410 Sqn scored his only kills (in NF XIII HK366/RA-Q), as he later recalled;

'I closed the range to 1200 ft through violent evasive action and identified a Do 217 using the Ross night glasses. I closed in to 400 ft astern and below, pulled the nose of the Mosquito up and fired two short bursts. The target's port engine and wing disintegrated in a flash of orange flame.'

The Dornier crashed into the ground beneath Price and his navigator, Plt Off J G Costello, and the pair duly continued their patrol southeast of Caen. Costello had soon gained another contact about two miles away, and it was quickly identified as a second Do 217. This was despatched as quickly as the first one. A further two bombers fell to No 410 Sqn's guns in what was an outstanding night for the unit.

The following night, 13 June, one of No 264 Sqn's flight commanders continued his route to 'acedom'. Flt Lt Ivor Cosby was at the controls of NF XIII HK502 with Flt Lt E R Murphy about 25 miles north of the Normandy beaches when, at around 0200 hrs, they were sent southeast by GCI towards a possible target flying at about 6000 ft. Cosby recalled what happened next;

'Two minutes later, several contacts appeared dead ahead at a range of just three miles. All closed rapidly on us, which suggested that I was flying into "window", whereupon I felt myself passing through an aircraft's slipstream. My "nav" gave me hard port, and shortly afterwards gained contact one-and-a-half miles ahead and well above. Our contact was continuously turning and throwing out "window" as I closed and obtained a visual. It was an extremely dark, moonless night, with ten-tenths cloud above, and identification was very difficult as the target appeared simply as a dark blob. When almost directly below it, we identified the aircraft as an He 177, at which point my "nav" sat back, folded his hands on his lap and prepared to enjoy the fun!

'I climbed up behind the Heinkel, closed to 200 yards and fired a one second burst. There was a blinding yellow flash, with red sparks around the port wing root and cockpit – debris flew off and I broke away to port. I saw the Heinkel well below me on my starboard side crossing to port, rapidly losing height, and with flames pouring from it. I throttled right back, passing right over it, when the bomber blew up with a huge flash.'

A Battle of Britain veteran who had flown Spitfires with several units during the summer of 1940, Cosby had subsequently seen action in Defiants and Beaufighters with No 141 Sqn. Posted to No 264 Sqn as a flight commander in September 1943, he would claim four Mosquito victories to add to his successes in Spitfires and Beaufighters.

Two hours after Cosby got his He 177, fellow No 264 Sqn pilot and nine-victory Beaufighter ace Flt Lt Michael Davison destroyed a Ju 88 – the first of his four kills with the Mosquito.

INCREASED BOMBER ACTIVITY

The Luftwaffe now sortied large numbers of aircraft in a futile attempt to disrupt the invasion, allowing most of the Mosquito squadrons to regularly make claims. Soon after midnight on 14 June, Flt Lt Bob Cowper and Flg Off Bill Watson of the Australian-manned No 456 Sqn

CHAPTER THREE

Sqn Ldr Bob Cowper (right) and Flt Lt Bill Watson (left) were an outstanding team with No 456 Sqn RAAF, claiming four enemy bombers destroyed during the summer of 1944. These victories took the young Australian pilot's total to six, but, frustratingly, further action eluded him (*J W Bennett*)

were patrolling off the French coast when they gained a freelance contact on a climbing target over the western tip of the Cherbourg peninsula. They observed no 'window' and opened fire from a distance of 400 ft with a one-and-a-half-second burst, having identified their target as a Ju 88 flying at 12,000 ft. There was a large flash and much debris, and three of the crew were seen to bale out as the bomber spun into the sea. Having already claimed two Beaufighter kills with No 108 Sqn over Sicily in 1943 and an He 177 and a Do 217 over the invasion beaches on 9/10 June, 22 year-old Bob Cowper had now achieved his magical fifth victory.

That night No 264 Sqn's Flt Lt John Corre destroyed a 'Ju 88 composite with an Me 109' – clearly one of the new *Mistel* combinations – for his fourth, and last, victory. Twenty-four hours later No 219 Sqn ace Flt Lt Mike Gloster got his sixth victory when he destroyed a Ju 88 whilst flying NF XVII HK315. This was his first kill with the Mosquito, having claimed his previous five victories on Beaufighters with No 255 Sqn in North Africa in 1942-43.

On 16/17 June No 488 Sqn's Sqn Ldr Nigel Bunting got his ninth, and last, kill (his fifth since joining the squadron) when he shot down an Fw 190 near St Lo. Another successful pilot who made his final claims over the beachheads – on 18/19 June – was No 125 Sqn's CO, Wg Cdr Johnny Topham, with long-standing navigator Flt Lt H W Berridge. In his combat report he recalled;

'We were at 8000 ft (in NF XVII HK346/VA-D) and contact was obtained at four miles slightly below and climbing. We rapidly closed in and obtained a visual at 800 yards as we approached from below and obtained a plan view of a Ju 88 with two external bombs inboard of the engines. We then closed and I fired a burst – many strikes were seen and smoke and bits came off the starboard engine and fuselage. It continued to fly straight, losing height while still going north, so I closed in and fired a short burst. The wing tip fell off and it immediately turned on its back and fell vertically, with the port wing on fire. It hit the sea and exploded.

'After a few minutes we received a vector and gained visual contact with another Ju 88 with external bomb racks at 400 yards. We closed in and I fired a short burst. It immediately exploded and went down vertically in three pieces, all in flames, striking the sea, where it continued to burn.'

These victories took Topham's final tally to 14.

Another experienced pilot, albeit one to whom success had been frustratingly elusive, was 34-year-old Sqn Ldr John Chase of No 264 Sqn, who, in the early hours of 20 June, finally broke his duck, as he later recalled;

'I was patrolling north of the beachhead at 8000 ft and was told of some "window" about. At 0330 hrs my navigator (Plt Off A F Watson) picked

In a shot clearly posed for the attendant press photographer, Flg Offs Jack Haddon (right) and Ralph McIlvenny are seen at Colerne just after D-Day with Mosquito NF XIII MM465/NG-X in the background. Although Haddon only claimed four kills (two of which were with No 604 Sqn in 1943, flying Mosquitoes), his DFC citation credited him with five victories! MM465 was the personal aircraft of Haddon's squadron CO, Wg Cdr Michael Constable-Maxwell, who claimed his final two victories and a probable in it during July 1944. This aircraft subsequently served with No 264 Sqn and was struck off charge in August 1947 (*via J D Oughton*)

up a contact just over two miles away at "two o'clock". I turned gently to port and closed very rapidly, obtaining a visual slightly to port and above. I closed in to 100 yards, astern and slightly below, and identified it as a Ju 88, which was still turning gently to port at 200 mph. I drew back and gave it a one-and-a-half-second burst. No strikes were seen, but it dived steeply to port. I was able to follow for a while, and the navigator saw it going down, throwing out sparks and flames.'

Although the crew did not see their victim crash, their controller assured them shortly afterwards that it had come down, allowing Chase to claim the first of his five victories.

Four nights later, on 24/25 June, young New Zealander Flg Off 'Jamie' Jameson of Zeals-based No 488 Sqn claimed a Me 410 in NF XIII MM466 for his first Mosquito victory – he had previously scored three kills flying Beaufighters with No 125 Sqn in 1942-43. Jameson 'made ace' by month-end, and he would go on to score a total of eight Mosquito victories (including no fewer than four on 29/30 July).

Veteran nightfighter unit No 604 Sqn, based at Colerne, also saw plenty of action during this period. One of its most successful pilots in the spring and early summer of 1944 was the unit's battle-seasoned CO, Wg Cdr Michael Constable-Maxwell. Having scored his first kills as long ago as May 1940 whilst flying Hurricane Is with No 56 Sqn, he had claimed his first Mosquito nightfighter successes as a flight commander with No 264 Sqn in early 1943. Constable-Maxwell, who had previously served with No 604 Sqn in 1941, rejoined his old unit as its CO in April 1943 and claimed his first (day) kill with the squadron four months later.

Having destroyed two Ju 188s in March and May 1944, Constable-Maxwell, flying with his navigator Flt Lt John Quinton, needed just one more victory to achieve 'acedom'. Knowing that their tour was rapidly coming to an end, they desperately sought out that elusive fifth victory over France. On the night of 2/3 July the crew was sent to patrol over Cherbourg in NF XIII MM465/NG-X, and they soon detected a Ju 88 flying over Ouistreham at about 3000 ft. Constable-Maxwell explained what happened next;

'We slightly overshot, and were dead underneath and slightly in front of the Ju 88. We broke away hard to port and then back to starboard, and he did the same thing and we nearly collided! We again turned to port, and the bomber commenced a gentle dive towards a patch of dark sea. We immediately turned back and gave it a long burst from slightly above and at 250 yards. There was a big white explosion, and as I broke away to starboard, we saw a cloud of black smoke as it went down steeply. We broke away, and after a tight orbit, saw a fire below in the sea.'

Constable-Maxwell had scored his fifth victory, and he followed this up with another Ju 88 (and a Do 217 probable) on the night of 8/9 July.

In spite of losses such as these, the Luftwaffe continued to send bombers against the invasion beachhead, recognising that the Allied armies' vulnerable logistics 'tail' was still dependent on the stores being offloaded from vessels just offshore. Mosquito nightfighter crews experienced almost nightly contacts as a result, allowing most squadrons to enjoy numerous aerial successes. Among them was No 604 Sqn, which had welcomed ace Wg Cdr Desmond Hughes as its new CO following Constable-Maxwell's final, successful, sortie on 8/9 July. In the wake of the latter's departure, one of his officers noted, 'We were sorry to see him go – he was a great character and friend, and on his last night he got a Hun to bring 604's night "bag" to 100'.

Another unit experiencing a change of command during July was No 406 Sqn, based at Winkleigh, which on the 27th saw flight commander 'Blackie' Williams take over the reigns following his promotion to wing commander. The unit had been partially equipped with Mosquitoes since April, but in August its remaining Beaufighter VIFs were replaced with new NF XXXs. Williams had been flying one of these (MM731) off the coast of Brittany on 21 July when the destroyer force that he had been tasked with covering came under attack from two

The Mosquito's cramped cockpit is clearly evident in this photograph, with No 604 Sqn's CO, Wg Cdr Michael Constable-Maxwell, at the controls, and his navigator, Flt Lt John Quinton, sat beside him (*via M Bowman*)

Do 217s at low level. 'Making ace' during the course of the action which ensued, he later recalled his one-sided clash with the bombers for the squadron's history book;

'I closed to 100 yards and noticed what appeared to be torpedoes slung beneath the fuselages. I opened fire at a distance to attract their attention – they were flying in echelon, and both opened fire at me. I closed on the starboard one and attacked, striking his port engine, which caught fire and exploded. The Dornier turned on its back and crashed into the sea.

'Just then we noticed our starboard engine streaming white smoke, with the radiator temperature off the clock, so it was immediately feathered, but we found one Dornier still ahead of us. As we were going home anyway, I closed on my one engine and opened fire. His port engine exploded and he started diving steeply to starboard – I noticed one of the crew bale out and the rest starting to climb onto the wings. Just before it crashed, and when at about 100 ft, another Mosquito attacked, causing it to disintegrate and hit the sea in flames.'

HIGHS AND LOWS FOR NO 488 SQN

Nightfighting was, however, hazardous, and on the night of 29 July No 488 Sqn suffered a severe blow when nine-victory ace Sqn Ldr Nigel Bunting and his navigator Flt Lt C P Reed were shot down and killed by flak. That same night squadronmates 'Jamie' Jameson and Norman Crookes were on patrol over Caen in NF XIII MM466/ME-R on what became possibly the finest nightfighter sortie of the Normandy campaign. The 22-year-old Kiwi wrote in his combat report;

'I obtained a visual on a Ju 88 (Ju 88A-4 B3+BH of I./KG 54) head on at one mile, and at the same height, against the dawn. I turned hard to port after it, following on AI as it skimmed through the cloud tops. I closed in at full throttle, and regaining visual, closed in and gave it two short bursts from dead astern. Strikes were seen, causing a fire in the fuselage and port engine. It went down through the clouds vertically, well alight, and hit the ground with a terrific explosion.

'I then went into a port orbit, and a contact was obtained almost immediately, followed quickly after by a visual. This aircraft was also skimming the cloud tops. I gave chase to overtake it, but then another Ju 88 came up through the cloud a mile ahead of us. I closed rapidly and confirmed it as a Ju 88, but its pilot appeared to see me and turned hard, diving towards thick cloud. I followed and closed to 300 yards, when I opened fire. Strikes caused a very large fire in the starboard engine, and it was well alight when it disappeared vertically though cloud.'

Initially, Jameson claimed this aircraft as a probable, but it was subsequently confirmed destroyed. He and Crookes then encountered two other Mosquitoes, before Jameson spotted another target;

In the early hours of 30 July 1944, 22-year-old New Zealander Flt Lt 'Jamie' Jameson (right) and his navigator, Flg Off Norman Crookes (left), shot down three Ju 88s and a Do 217 in the aircraft parked behind them – MM466/ME-R, in which they eventually claimed eight kills! Jameson was the most successful New Zealand nightfighter pilot of the war (*P H T Green collection*)

CHAPTER THREE

With 18 and one shared victories, No 604 Sqn's Wg Cdr Desmond Hughes was one of the RAF's most successful nightfighter pilots, although only his final two kills were claimed on the Mosquito. The first of these came in NF XIII MM465, which can be seen in the photograph on page 29 (*via G R Pitchfork*)

Another outstanding sortie of the summer of 1944 was flown by Flt Lt John Surman of No 604 Sqn, who, on the evening of 6 August, downed two Do 217s and a Bf 110G nightfighter to become an ace. The latter was flown by 36-victory *experte* Oberleutnant Helmut Bergmann, *Staffelkapitan* of 8./NJG 4 (*J C Surman*)

'I closed to dead astern and identified it as a Ju 88, which was confirmed by my navigator. When I was about 300 yards astern of the enemy aircraft, it dived steeply towards cloud. I followed, and gave the bomber two short bursts and saw strikes on the fuselage. I followed using AI, although it was taking violent evasive action and dropping large quantities of "window". At almost treetop height, visual was regained dead astern, so I closed in and gave it a short burst. It pulled up almost vertically, with debris and sparks falling from it, and nose-dived into a field and exploded.'

Having reported this kill, the crew was vectored back towards further enemy activity, spotting two aircraft. Jameson continued;

'I decided to intercept the nearer and obtained a visual on a Do 217, which must have seen me for it immediately dived into cloud and took violent evasive action. I followed through cloud using AI, and it eventually straightened out at the cloud base. Visual was regained and I closed and fired a short burst, after which the fuselage began to burn furiously. It turned gently to starboard, pulled its nose up and dived into the ground in flames and exploded.'

In very poor weather Jameson and Crookes had brought down four enemy bombers. In early August, having taken his total to 11, Jameson was repatriated home following a request by his mother, who had already lost two sons during the conflict and had just been left a widow following the sudden death of her husband. Jameson returned to Rotherham, in New Zealand, to take over the running of the family farm.

No 604 Sqn also continued to be active from its base at Colerne, and on 3 August Flt Lt Jack 'Fingers' Foster and his navigator Flg Off Maurice 'Ping' Newton were on patrol in NF XIII MM552/NG-N just after 2300 hrs near Granville in clear, fine weather. The pair, who had previously gained four victories on Beaufighters with Nos 604 and 108 Sqns, were vectored onto a contact, as Jack Foster later recounted;

'I pulled the nose up and fired a two-second burst from 150 yards as it turned gently starboard, and strikes were seen. A second burst resulted in a blinding flash from the fuselage and port engine. It then dived, firing from a belly position, and we followed. We thought he was finished, however, at 5000 ft he levelled off and I tried another burst, although the gun-sight had gone out. Flashes were seen on the fuselage, and as it dived to port we were engaged by friendly AA that hit our port engine, wing and the cabin roof. I fired a burst, "hose-piping" as best I could, but at 2500 ft I pulled out due to heavy ack ack.'

The wreckage of a Do 217 that crashed at about 2325 hrs was found south of Granville, so Jack Foster was credited with his fifth victory – also his first of five on the Mosquito. That same night No 604 Sqn's sister unit within the 2nd TAF, No 264 Sqn, also gained a success when Flt Lt Ivor Cosby, in NF XIII PS-S, claimed the last of four and one shared victories;

'I was on patrol just south of Vize under "Yardley" control, who put me onto a bogey about 15 miles away. I saw the target crossing below, port to starboard, and identified a Ju 88. I at once closed to attack, and it started very violent evasive action. I was quite unable to turn inside him, so I did an upward half-roll and aileron turned onto him, giving him a short burst and hit the starboard wing tip. I gave him another short burst and saw a small explosion at the rear of the fuselage, so I gave him a third burst.

There was an explosion outboard of the port engine and flames streamed back to a distance of about 150 ft. There were three distinct explosions and it struck the ground.'

Two days later, on 6 August, Desmond Hughes led No 604 Sqn to the captured airfield at A 8 Picauville, thus giving the unit the distinction of being the first Mosquito nightfighter squadron to be based on the Continent. That night he celebrated the move by opening No 604 Sqn's Continental scorebook by bringing down a Ju 88 near Avranches while flying NF XIII MM465. Also on patrol that night was squadronmate John Surman, who told the Author;

'We were given a vector towards a bogey 15 miles away. My navigator, "Paddy" Weston, obtained a contact well below to port. The target did an orbit against the moon as we gained visual on a Bf 110, allowing me to close to within 600 ft of the target, at which distance I gave it a two-second burst. I saw an explosion in the engines and fuselage and it dropped out of the sky and exploded upon hitting the ground. Having completed my first bit of action, I returned to the airwaves to find "Hoops" in trouble.

'"Hoops", did you get him?" "Yes, but he got me."

'"Are you happy?" "No!"

'"Hoops" then came to me with questions. "Can you see a large fire? We are near water . . . they are firing at me!" Then silence.'

Veteran nightfighter pilot Flt Lt John Hooper, who had four Beaufighter and Mosquito kills to his name, had damaged an Me 410 in NF XIII MM621. His machine was in turn hit either by the Messerschmitt's defensive fire or flak, and he crashed to his death with his navigator, Flg Off S C 'Mum' Hubbard. Surman continued;

'We were then sent north to resume our patrol, being given a vector towards a contact that my navigator picked up on AI slightly above in a port orbit. I closed in gradually to directly below, and identified a

On the night that John Surman became an ace, Flt Lt John Hooper engaged Bf 110G-4 Wk-Nr 440125/3C+ES, flown by Feldwebel Günther Zimmermann, in combat. Sadly, Hooper's Mosquito NF XIII (MM621) was hit either by return fire from the Bf 110 or flak, and it crashed in Normandy. He was credited with a damaged, which was his fifth score, but sadly both Hooper and Flg Off S C Hubbard died in the subsequent crash. They were buried in Bayeux War Cemetery (*J C Surman*)

Do 217, its black crosses on the wings being clearly visible. I drew up astern and gave it a burst – the starboard engine exploded and the bomber dived vertically to starboard, exploding as it hit the ground.

'We returned to our patrol area, and whilst being vectored home, the controller requested I investigate an aircraft ahead. I turned and closed in slowly, identifying the aircraft from beneath as another Do 217. I drew up and gave it a short burst, after which the port engine exploded but did not catch fire. I then overshot. I turned hard to port, came in again and saw it flying on one engine, with smoke coming from the other. I fired a couple more bursts and again the port engine exploded. Overshooting, I came round for a third attack. I fired another burst, overshot and did a tight orbit to come in again.

'By this time we were down to 2000 ft, and I fired, overshot, turned hard to port and saw its port engine on fire. The bomber then dived hard, hit the ground and exploded.'

Johnny Surman's exploits during this epic sortie had made him an ace. He later discovered that his first victim was 36-victory *experte* Oberleutnant Helmut Bergmann, *Staffelkapitan* of 8./NJG 4, who perished with his crew in Bf 110G-4 Wk-Nr 140320/3C+CS.

On the night of 7/8 August, Flt Lt Michael Davison of No 264 Sqn shot down a Ju 88 for his 12th, and final, kill, while on the 10th his flight commander, Sqn Ldr John Chase, also reached 'acedom' with a Ju 188 destroyed east of Le Havre. Four days later the unit joined No 604 Sqn at Picauville to provide integral night defence to the Allied armies.

Other 2nd TAF units that remained based in England also continued to be active, including No 488 Sqn at Colerne under Wg Cdr Dickie Haine, who, at 2330 hrs on 1 September, scored his final success of the war, having made his first claim in November 1939 when flying Blenheim IFs with No 25 Sqn. He recalled the event for the Author;

'We were flying (NF XIII MM566/ME-A) in very bright moonlight west of the French coast when I saw an aircraft silhouetted against the moonbeam on the sea. I found a Ju 188 right above me going the other way! I hauled round and opened up more or less straight away, although I believe that the gun-sight was unserviceable. Nevertheless, I managed some hits on the right engine and debris came back, which I avoided, before attacking again, after which it just went straight into the sea.'

The V1 Campaign

One of the enemy responses to the invasion was the launching of large numbers of V1 flying bombs at southern England from sites in the Pas de Calais area, although many of these had been attacked during the first half of 1944. Still more 'Doodlebugs' were air-launched from He 111s operating in the Cherbourg area, these weapons generally being aimed at Southampton and other south coast ports.

Although the small unmanned, pulse-jet powered aircraft were usually inaccurate, they nevertheless posed a clear threat to cities in the south of England. The first seven were launched on 10 June, and they prompted an immediate response. The first one to fall to a Mosquito was credited on the night of the 14th to Flt Lt John Musgrave of No 605 Sqn. Crashing into the central Channel, it was the first of 12 he would destroy flying FB VIs, thus making him a V1 ace.

No 96 Sqn was led by the very capable Wg Cdr Edward Crew during 1944, the ace claiming 21 V1s destroyed as well as three aircraft. The latter took Crew's final total to 12 and one shared destroyed (*via C F Shores*)

As well as large numbers of ADGB day fighter units, several Mosquito nightfighter squadrons were also tasked with performing 'anti-diver' duties at various times through the coming months. These included Nos 96, 125, 219 and 456 Sqns from ADGB, as well as the intruders from Nos 418 and 605 Sqns. The 2nd TAF's Nos 264 and 604 Sqns were also switched to anti-V1 operations, and Nos 85 and 157 Sqns were pulled from No 100 Group's bomber support campaign in July and based at West Malling for a month in order to participate in these missions.

At Ford, No 96 Sqn was in the forefront of the night anti-V1 defences, and the unit was eventually to become the top scoring nightfighter squadron, and the fourth highest destroyer of 'Doodlebugs' overall with around 180 downed.

Although the V1s were pilotless, and therefore unable to evade interception, the task of shooting them down was no easy matter, as No 96 Sqn's CO, Wg Cdr Edward Crew explained to the Author;

'The V1 was a small, fast target – it normally flew at 400 mph at about 2000 ft. To catch it in a Mosquito, it was necessary to do a steep diving turn onto the flying bomb, aiming to be within firing range at the bottom of the dive. The prospects of catching it in straight and level flight were not good. At night, it was difficult to judge the range of the single exhaust flame, although at the optimum distance – about 100 yards – it was possible to discern the red hot engine tube. If the warhead was hit, the V1 blew up, and we inevitably flew through the explosion – one pilot reported a red-hot engine flying past him!

'In an attempt to improve the maximum speed of our aircraft, the Merlins were uprated to give a maximum of +25 lbs boost pressure using 150 octane fuel. This led to a number of engine failures, one of which occurred when the uprated engine was being demonstrated to a Rolls-Royce representative!'

Nonetheless, the squadron was highly successful, and Crew himself shot down 21 V1s to add to the 12 and one shared aircraft that he had shot down, including three on the Mosquito. He claimed his first 'diver' north of Dungeness on 20 June when flying MM499/VJ-V, but four nights later, when over the Channel south of Hastings in the same aircraft, the exploding flying bomb so damaged the Mosquito that Crew and his navigator had to bale out.

The most successful 'anti-diver' Mosquito pilot of them all was fellow ace Flg Off F R L 'Togs' Mellersh, who already had seven victories from his Beaufighter days with No 600 Sqn in North Africa in 1943. The son of a World War 1 Sopwith Triplane and Camel ace, he joined No 96 Sqn just as the V1 campaign began. Mellersh claimed his first 'Doodlebug' whilst flying MM577/ZJ-N on 20 June, and became a V1 ace a week later when he and his navigator, Flg Off Michael Stanley, brought down four in a night.

During an incredible mission on 3 August, Mellersh was thought to have established an RAF record for V1s destroyed during a single sortie when he brought down nine! His last V1 was destroyed on 23 September, taking Mellersh's overall tally to at least 39, and possibly as many as 42.

The Cambridgeshire-based No 25 Sqn also saw action against the V1s, as detailed by Flt Lt Alfred Marshall following a sortie in the early hours of 16 August;

East coast-based No 68 Sqn spent the last months of the war countering the threat of air-launched V1s, with Mosquito NF XXX NT531/WM-T flying its first such sortie in the hands of Flt Lt Talbot on 4 April 1945. Serving with No 157 Sqn post-war, this aircraft was transferred to the *Armée de l'Air* in May 1948 (*I Simpson*)

'I was airborne on an "anti-diver" patrol and saw three flying bombs coming – two at 8000 ft and the other at about 2000 ft. I saw another at 2000-3000 ft, travelling at about 360 mph. I dived and attacked, opening fire from approximately 300 yards. After the first burst the radar went unserviceable, and it was difficult to judge range. As I turned away, I saw the flying bomb explode in the air.'

In early September the Allied armies overran the launch areas and the attacks ceased. However, within two weeks V1s were being air-launched over the North Sea at night from He 111H bombers operating from Dutch bases. By the end of September a total of 80 had been launched, although many of these had been destroyed. The main counter to the launch aircraft came from the Coltishall-based Mosquitoes of Nos 25 and 68 Sqns.

Czech Beaufighter ace Sqn Ldr Miro Mansfeld of No 68 Sqn shot an air-launched V1 down on 24 October, while on the evening of 6 November, No 25 Sqn's Alfred Marshall was sent out on an anti-V1 patrol and found a launch He 111. He wrote in his report;

'Shortly after commencing my patrol I saw a flying bomb released and soon obtained visual and identified an He 111. It was at a height of 600 ft, so I pulled up and opened fire with a two-second burst. An explosion occurred in the port wing and the aircraft disintegrated.'

This kill took Marshall's final wartime tally to 16 and two shared victories in the air and 17 destroyed on the ground, the bulk of which had come whilst flying Hurricanes with No 73 Sqn and Kittyhawks with No 250 Sqn in France and North Africa. Tragically, he and his navigator were killed three weeks later on 27 November when their Mosquito hit the ground during a low-level beat-up of Coltishall upon their return from a mission.

Fellow No 25 Sqn ace Flt Lt Douglas Greaves downed a 'carrier' just after midnight on 11 November for his ninth, and final, victory, as he related to the Author for this volume;

'We found an He 111 at 200 ft, opened fire with a long burst from dead astern and a sheet of flame was seen from the starboard engine and wing root. We climbed and the Heinkel glided slowly into the sea.'

Mosquito NF XXX MT487/ZK-L saw lengthy service with No 25 Sqn, and during the autumn of 1944 it was regularly flown by several notable pilots, including aces Flt Lts Douglas Greaves and Alfred Marshall. In the hands of Flt Lt F M Slater, the aircraft also flew No 25 Sqn's final war sorties the following spring. MT487 was struck off charge in August 1948, having served exclusively with No 25 Sqn (*J D R Rawlings*)

On 24 August 1944, No 409 Sqn's Mosquito NF XIIIs arrived in France at B 17 Carpiquet, from where MM512 is seen taxiing out two days later. It was flown during the summer by future ace Flg Off Ralph Britten, but was lost to flak near Ostend on 7 October (*Canadian Forces*)

These air-launched attacks continued on a small scale until the following spring. By then no fewer than 25 Mosquito pilots had become V1 aces, as well as a further eight who were also full aerial aces too.

Action over the Continent

With the French airfield at Picauville affected by heavy rain in early September, No 264 Sqn moved to B 6 Coulombs. A few days later No 604 Sqn also departed for B 17 Carpiquet, where, on the 24th, it was replaced by No 409 Sqn and transferred back to Predannack for a rest, soon to be followed by No 264 Sqn. Forty-eight hours earlier, No 410 Sqn had arrived at B 48 Amiens/Glisy.

One of the unit's pilots was flight commander Sqn Ldr Dean Somerville, who had claimed four victories in the first two weeks of August to add to his previous claim in February to 'make ace' shortly before the move.

Gradually, more 2nd TAF Mosquito squadrons were sent to the Continent, and these, in company with their UK-based brethren, roamed the night skies of France, the Low Countries and, increasingly, Germany. Indeed as the Luftwaffe's night offensive capability waned, the delineation between Mosquito nightfighter, intruder and bomber support squadrons became increasing blurred.

The 2nd TAF's newest Mosquito nightfighter unit was No 219 Sqn, which made its first claim since joining on 12 September when Flt Lt

NF XIII MM571 of No 264 Sqn closes on another Mosquito as it heads out on patrol. The aircraft's first sortie with the squadron was performed on the day of the Allied airborne landings in Holland (17 September 1944), when it was flown by ace Flt Lt Ken Rayment (*L Hunt*)

Leslie Stephenson shot down a Ju 88 over the Dutch border for the eighth of his ten victories (six where claimed flying Beaufighters with No 153 Sqn in North Africa in 1943). Soon afterwards his CO, Wg Cdr Peter Green, who was flying with the RAF's most successful nightfighter navigator, Flt Lt Douglas Oxby, shot down a Bf 110 near Cologne for his sixth victory. Oxby participated in 21 successful interceptions, and ended the war with a DSO, DFC and DFM.

The Allied airborne invasion of Holland and the subsequent reverse at Arnhem led to an upsurge in activity in the area, particularly in German efforts to destroy the recently captured bridges. One of those units to benefit from this was No 410 Sqn, which had only just made the move from England to Amiens/Glisy. Squadron pilot Lt Archie Harrington claimed his first kill on the evening of 26 September, when, in bright moonlight, he shot down a Ju 87 north of Aachen in NF XXX MM743;

'I dropped back to approximately 300 ft and opened fire. Strikes were observed on the wing root and fuselage, and the undercarriage was blown off. We followed the enemy aircraft around and gave it two additional bursts. It passed under my wing and exploded violently on the ground, where it was seen burning very nicely.'

This was Harrington's third victory, and he became the leading USAAF nightfighter pilot on 25 November in the action depicted on the cover of this volume.

Another Stuka was shot down by future nine-kill ace Flt Lt G R I 'Sailor' Parker of No 219 Sqn on 28 September. Having previously destroyed six V1s, this Ju 87 took the former wireless operator/gunner's tally to four, and the squadron's to exactly 100. Parker's CO went two better on 2 October when, again with Oxby, Wg Cdr Green shot down three Stukas east of Nijmegen. The squadron moved to Amiens a week later to join No 147 Wing, and in mid November No 488 Sqn also arrived at the French airfield. From there, both units regularly flew patrols into Germany, where crews discovered just how disconcerting it was to be caught in searchlights – something they were not used to!

THE BATTLE OF THE BULGE

The 2nd TAF's nightfighter units were usually held on standby for 48 hours at a time, then stood down for the next 48. The routine was disrupted somewhat in early December by the onset of bad weather, which kept both Allied and German aircraft firmly on the ground. This changed in the middle of the month, however, with the launching of a surprise Wehrmacht offensive (later named the Battle of the Bulge) in the

During its time on the Continent, No 219 Sqn was led by Wg Cdr Peter Green. A highly successful nightfighter pilot who increased his score to 14 destroyed during his tenure, he was killed whilst air-testing a Mosquito shortly before the end of the war (*via C F Shores*)

The Mosquito NF XXXs of No 410 Sqn await their next sorties at Amiens/Glisy during the autumn of 1944. The nearest one is MM788/RA-Q, which was the regular aircraft of Flt Lt Walter Dinsdale. He claimed the last of his three victories in it on 27 December. The Mosquito was also flown on occasion by six-victory ace Flt Lt 'Pop' Edinger (*D Tongue*)

No 409 Sqn's NF XIII HK425/KP-R was named *Lonesome Polecat* by its crew of Flg Offs Ross Finlayson and Al Webster, who downed a Ju 88 with it on 18 December 1944. HK425 had previously destroyed an Me 410, and when serving with No 96 Sqn earlier in the year, Flt Lt Kennedy had shot down a Ju 88 (*R Finlayson*)

Flt Lt K W Stewart (right) and his navigator, Flg Off H E Brumby, of No 488 Sqn pose in front of their NF XXX NT263, which shows the 5.5 victory symbols that the crew claimed between December 1944 and April 1945. Three of these came in NT263 (*author's collection*)

Ardennes under the cover of dreadful weather. This in turn led to an upsurge in enemy air activity as the weather improved, and the Mosquito squadrons enjoyed a number of successes.

On the evening of the 18th, No 410 Sqn's Flt Lt C E 'Pop' Edinger (an American in the RCAF) and Flg Off C C Vaessen, flying NF XXX MV527, were vectored onto a contact by mobile GCI station 'Rejoice' near the Belgian-Dutch border. The crew eventually identified a Ju 88, and as it turned to the right, Edinger later stated in his combat report;

'I fired a short burst, scoring strikes and starting a small fire in the starboard engine. He went down under my starboard wing, but we were unable to follow as we were very low at approximately 200 ft – my navigator could see the trees. It was seen to hit the ground and explode.'

This was Edinger's fifth victory, so making him a member of the elite band of nightfighter aces. His final success came on Christmas Eve when he destroyed a Ju 87 again while flying MV527.

The 'newcomers' of No 219 Sqn were also active during this period, with the Green/Oxby combination claiming a Ju 88 on 23/24 December and a Ju 87 two days later. Two other aces serving with the unit also increased their scores at this time, 'Sailor' Parker bagging two Ju 188s over Holland on 23/24 December and Flt Lt Leslie Stephenson a Bf 110 over western Germany two nights later for his tenth, and last, kill.

The squadron diarist noted December as 'a good month for the squadron overall!', and 1945 started in a similar vein for No 219 Sqn when, on New Year's Day, Flt Lt Reynolds quickly opened the squadron's 1945 account when he shot down a Bf 110.

Despite the war in Europe now entering its final phase, Mosquito

Having scored several successes in 1943 flying Beaufighter VIFs with No 108 Sqn in the Mediterranean, Flt Lts Reg Foster (left) and 'Apple' Newton (right) returned to the UK to claim five victories over western Europe in the Mosquito NF XIII during a tour with No 604 Sqn. Three of these kills (a trio of Ju 88G nightfighters) fell to the pair in the early hours of New Year's Day 1945 (*via G R Pitchfork*)

crews were still faced with many hazards whilst operating over enemy territory, not the least of which were the ever-effective light flak batteries scattered across the country. The NF XXX of No 488 Sqn's Flt Lt K W 'Chunky' Stewart and Flg Off H E 'Bill' Brumby was hit by flak when chasing Ju 87s on 27 December, and four days later their fighter was again badly shot up by flak defences surrounding the Luftwaffe nightfighter base at Rheine while stalking an enemy aircraft. With his hydraulics shot away, future five-kill ace Stewart successfully landed at Brussels just before the massed enemy attack codenamed Operation *Bodenplatte* hit the airfield, which was soon littered with burning aircraft. Somehow, their crippled Mosquito escaped further damage.

The previous day, No 604 Sqn had returned from England, and Flt Lts Reg Foster and 'Ping' Newton (in NF XIII HK526) claimed their squadron's first kill for 1945 in spectacular style on 1/2 January during a patrol from Lille/Vendeville under the control of 'Voicebox' GCI. Foster later recalled the highlights of the mission in his combat report;

'We closed in to a position almost vertically underneath, staying until we had identified the target as a Ju 88 (a Ju 88G, which was the fighter version fitted with BMW engines). I throttled back and pulled up the nose into a firing position and fired a two-second burst at 100 yards. Strikes were seen all over the fuselage, which temporarily blinded me, so I pulled away to starboard. I then saw it above to port, crossing in a shallow dive, and gave him a short burst, seeing more strikes before he fell away under my starboard wing. I orbited, and after a few seconds saw the Ju 88 explode in flame.'

The pair then investigated another contact at 7000 ft and soon sent their second Ju 88G down to crash in a mass of flames just 20 minutes after the first. They were then sent after several intermittent low contacts and eventually 'identified a Ju 88 with the starboard prop feathered. I pulled up and opened fire from dead astern at 100 yards, hitting the fuselage and port engine. Three parachutes appeared immediately and passed close to us. It then dived vertically to explode on the ground'.

These three victories were Foster's last, taking his total to nine destroyed. His CO, Wg Cdr Desmond Hughes, made his final claim 12 days later when, on 13/14 January, he shot down a Ju 88 near Rotterdam to take his total to 18 and one shared destroyed, 15 of them at night.

The 2nd TAF's nightfighters continued to make occasional claims through into February, during which time the long awaited Anglo-Canadian push through the Reichwald to the Rhine took place. The offensive was accompanied by increased fighting on the ground, and at night Allied troops were covered by patrols from Nos 488 and 219 Sqns. The latter unit suffered a great loss on 1 March, however, when its highly successful and charismatic CO, Wg Cdr Peter Green, was killed air-testing a Mosquito which crashed near Amiens.

Despite the fighting on the ground, there was relatively little reaction from the Luftwaffe until the actual crossing of the Rhine began on 24 March. The following night No 409 Sqn's Flt Lt Ralph Britten became the latest Mosquito pilot to become an ace when he shot down a Ju 88 whilst patrolling over the Dortmund area in NF XIII MM513/NG-J.

By this time both Nos 219 and 488 Sqns had detachments operating in Holland from B 77 Gilze-Rijen. It was from this base shortly before 2200 hrs on 26 March that Flt Lt John Hall and Plt Off Taylor (who was not his regular navigator) scrambled in NF XXX NT370/ME-P on what was to prove an eventful sortie. Some miles north of the town of Emmerich, they were vectored towards a contact, which they rapidly closed on as Hall later described;

'I obtained a visual on a Ju 88 at a height of 7000 ft and closed in to a dead astern position, and as I was overtaking rapidly I opened fire with a two-second burst at 400 yards, producing strikes all over the cockpit. It climbed very steeply and I pulled out to one side and climbed with him. I turned in behind again and gave another two-second burst from about 300 yards, setting his port engine on fire, but by this time it was going so slowly that it was impossible to keep behind him. Both engines were now alight, but I gave him a final one-second burst. As it blew up, I felt debris strike my aircraft. I then saw the burning wreckage hit the ground.'

The damage sustained by the Mosquito was serious, and the crew found themselves faced with numerous problems, as Hall continued;

'I spotted a thick stream of white vapour coming from the region of the port engine and two large holes just outboard of the port engine in the leading edge of the wing. Flames were coming from the cowling of the port engine, so I feathered it. We were then at 6000 ft. To maintain this height on the starboard engine, I found that it was necessary to use 16 inches of boost and 3000 revs. I called for an emergency homing and "Palmolive" took me to Gilze-Rijen base, which was about 70 miles west.

'Arriving over the base, I began a right-hand circuit at 3000 ft. On selecting undercarriage down, the aircraft started to swerve violently and to lose height rapidly. I selected up again and found that my height was only 500 ft. I informed Flying Control that I was going to make a crash-landing, finishing up just off the end of the runway. We got out through the top hatch. As soon as I switched off the starboard engine, it caught fire and the aircraft partially burnt out.'

On the evening of 26 March 1945, Flt Lt John Hall of No 488 Sqn shot down a Ju 88 near Emmerich to claim his eighth victory. He was flying Mosquito NF XXX NT370/ME-P at the time, and his nightfighter was struck by debris from the stricken bomber during the course of the engagement. Despite his aircraft being badly damaged, Hall managed to carry out a successful wheels-up landing at Gilze-Rijen, where, as can be seen, the Mosquito was partially burned out (*C H Goss*)

The Ju 88 was Hall's eighth, and final, success. The following few days saw the nightfighters claim over a dozen victories, plus two V1s after they had been launched from He 111s.

The Third Reich was now imploding, and although the 2nd TAF's Mosquito patrols ranged far and wide from a variety of bases, they were usually under mobile GCI control. One aircraft that found 'trade' on 7/8 April was No 488 Sqn NF XXX MT263, flown by Flt Lt 'Chunky' Stewart. The resulting action, which made the New Zealander an ace, is described here by his squadronmate Allott Gabites;

'"Chunky" and Bill (Brumby) were directed onto a "bogey" over the Ruhr. In the long chase that followed, the rear gunner in the Me 110 opened fire on the Mosquito several times, but "Chunky" was able to bring his sights to bear and fire his own guns. Presently, a small fire started in the tail of the Messerschmitt, which grew and grew until the enemy aircraft dived into the ground and exploded. Thus "Chunky", in a comparatively short time, had brought his score up to five enemy aircraft destroyed and one damaged. Recognition of this achievement was to come with the award of DFCs to both "Chunky" and Bill. They were to be the squadron's last aces.'

Despite the Luftwaffe being starved of fuel for its aircraft, the Mosquito squadrons continued making claims. One of those to enjoy success in the final months of the war in Europe was No 410 Sqn's Flt Lt Rayne Schultz, who had initially served with the unit from December 1942 through to March 1944, during which time he claimed four kills. Following a spell in Training Command, he rejoined No 410 Sqn in December 1944 and had claimed his all important fifth victory (a Ju 188) on 13/14 February in NF XIII HK429. A second Ju 188 fell to Schultz's guns on 10/11 April while patrolling over the Damme area of Germany in NF XXX MM744. The young Albertan claimed his final kills on 21/22 April when he destroyed two Ju 88s in NF XXX MV527 near Ferrbellen.

Two nights later, No 409 Sqn, having recently moved into B 108 at Rheine to become the first Mosquito nightfighter unit to be based on German soil, enjoyed great success. Flg Off Evert Hermansen got two Ju 87s near Ludwigslust and an Fw 190 over Wittenberg in NF XIII HK419/KP-D for his only successes in almost two years of frontline flying with the unit. That same night, Flg Off John Skelly (who was killed on 23 June 1945 in a flying accident involving NF XIII MM567) shot down two Ju 52/3ms in NF XIII HK506/KP-H. Plt Off Leslie got a third Junkers transport. On 24/25 April No 409 Sqn's Plt Off Len Fitchett (in NF XIII MM588/KP-T) doubled his wartime tally of kills when he brought down yet another Ju 52/3m that he intercepted over Konigsberg, while his CO, Wg Cdr Richard Hatton, shot down a large Ju 290 with NF XIII MM517/KP-S for his third, and last, kill.

These victories all helped make No 409 Sqn the top scoring 2nd TAF nightfighter unit since D-Day. Many of its victims were aircraft trying to flee the shambles of Germany and escape to Denmark and Norway, as instructed by the senior Nazi leadership. Such lumbering types presented easy pickings for the seasoned Mosquito crews at this late stage in the war.

One of the original 2nd TAF Mosquito units, No 264 Sqn, which was still based in Lille, claimed its final success at 2200 hrs on 25 April when, over the wreckage of Berlin, Plt Offs J Hutton and H E Burraston used NF XIII HK466 to shoot down a lone Fw 190. This was Jack Hutton's second kill, for he had claimed an Italian SM.79 bomber whilst flying Beaufighters with No 600 Sqn in the Mediterranean in 1943.

There had been a gradual reduction in the number of Mosquito nightfighter squadrons within both Fighter Command and the 2nd TAF in the final months of the war, and many more were disbanded in the aftermath of VE-Day. Despite often difficult operating conditions, the 2nd TAF Mosquito units had provided a high level of protection to the Allied armies, and their vulnerable logistics train, since the invasion. During this time these squadrons had achieved the best kill-loss ratio of any of the Command's fighter units. Likewise over England, the squadrons had maintained their vigil against a greatly reduced threat, but one that remained potent almost to the end thanks to the occasional night intruder raid and the presence of air-launched V1s.

FIGHTER-BOMBER ACES

The versatile Mosquito was extensively used for fighter-bomber and coastal strike duties, the prime purpose of these squadrons being to attack surface targets in occupied Europe (see *Osprey Combat Aircraft No 4 – Mosquito Bomber/Fighter-Bomber Units of World War 2* and *Osprey Combat Aircraft No 9 – Mosquito Fighter/Fighter-Bomber Units of World War 2* for further details).

A number of aces served with these units, and a few also claimed aerial victories while flying Mosquito FB VIs. This fighter-bomber variant formed the backbone of Bomber Command's No 2 Group from mid 1943 onwards, and the 2nd TAF's Nos 21, 464 and 487 Sqns also re-equipped with the type (replacing woefully inadequate Ventura I/IIs) in the late summer of that same year, becoming part of No 140 Airfield (later Wing). The second Wing, No 138, was established at Lasham on 14 October 1943 when No 613 Sqn began conversion to Mosquitoes from Mustang Is. Its CO was Battle of France/Britain Hurricane ace Wg Cdr Ken Blair, who flew the unit's first operational sortie on 19 December.

In the Mosquito the RAF had an ideal weapon for true precision strikes, one of the most spectacular of which was the attack on the prison at Amiens on 18 February 1944 in a desperate attempt to free members of the Resistance held there under sentence of death. No 487 Sqn RNZAF began the attack, led by the squadron's CO and nightfighter ace, Wg Cdr I S 'Blackie' Smith. In spite of the subsequent loss of two aircraft to marauding Fw 190s, the attack was brilliantly executed, and allowed 258 prisoners to escape.

Leading this trio of Mosquito FB VIs from No 487 Sqn, photographed on 29 February 1944, is MM417/EG-T flown by the unit's CO, Wg Cdr 'Blackie' Smith. He was also at the controls of this machine on 26 March when it was hit by flak whilst attacking a V1 site at Les Hayes, the ace having to subsequently make a wheels-up landing at Hunsdon (*RAF Thorney Island*)

CHAPTER THREE

The outstanding Mosquito fighter pilot in No 2 Group was the aggressive Wg Cdr Bob Braham (right), who usually flew with his long-time navigator, Sqn Ldr 'Sticks' Gregory (left). In the spring of 1944, whilst ostensibly serving as a staff officer, Braham claimed nine aircraft destroyed during a series of 'scrounged' Day *Ranger* sorties! (*via C F Shores*)

The following month another nightfighter ace with five victories (including two on Mosquitoes), Sqn Ldr Henry Bodien, joined No 21 Sqn and flew his first sortie on the 2nd when he performed a night intruder mission that saw him successfully bomb Montdidier airfield.

More significantly, having begun 'scrounging' sorties on 28 February, on 5 March the Wing Commander Night Operations at HQ No 2 Group, Wg Cdr 'Bob' Braham, flew another day intruder. Borrowing FB VI LR364/SY-E from No 613 Sqn, he and his old navigator 'Sticks' Gregory shot down an He 177 of 3./KG 100 over Chateaudun for Braham's 20th victory, and his first kill with the Mosquito. In his autobiography *Scramble*, Braham wrote;

'He was circling the airfield at 1000 ft. We stayed on the deck until the last minute. When about half-a-mile away, I pulled up in a gentle climbing turn so that the massive fuselage of the bomber was ahead of us – a beam shot. At the last minute the enemy realised that we were hostile and attempted to turn away, but it was too late. I tightened the turn a little to set the dot of my gun-sight ahead of the bomber to allow for the correct deflection, and pressed the button. I tightened the turn a little more to keep my sights on the now rapidly closing target.

'I had started firing at about 400 yards, and now at 100 yards, with the He 177 looking as big as a house, a stream of flame and smoke appeared below the nose of the aircraft. It reared up like a wounded animal, then winged over on its back and dived vertically into the ground. The explosion when it hit was like an oil tank blowing up – a huge ball of red flame and clouds of thick oily smoke. "My God!" was all I could say.'

Two more kills followed on 24 March (a Ju 52/3m and a W 34), and then a singleton (a Bu 131) on 4 April. Nine days later, while flying FB VI LR313/SM-B of No 305 Sqn, Braham got his fifth and sixth Mosquito kills (an He 111 and an Fw 58) during a *Ranger* to Aalborg, in Denmark.

In early May 1944 Battle of Britain Spitfire aces Flt Lts George 'Grumpy' Unwin and Joe Kilner commenced FB VI operations with No 613 Sqn and No 21 Sqn, respectively. Following in 'Bob' Braham's footsteps, fellow No 2 Group staff officer, and six-kill ace, Sqn Ldr Mike Herrick (who had seen combat in Europe with the RAF in 1940-41 and in the Pacific with the RNZAF in 1942-43) started flying operations with various FB VI units as well. He later joined No 305 Sqn as 'B' Flight commander. Another ace returning to the frontline in FB VIs (with No 107 Sqn) at this time was Flt Lt Tony Rippon, who had last seen combat on Malta in 1941 in Hurricanes.

Denmark was proving a fruitful hunting ground for Braham, who shot down a Ju 88 there on 7 May, but he had a fortunate escape five days later. With Gregory alongside, he had flown an intruder to Denmark in a No 107 Sqn aircraft (NS885), and just west of Aalborg he had spotted an Fw 190;

'At 600 yards dead astern I opened fire, but my shells fell short. For a second we hit his prop wash and wallowed dangerously. The tension in our aircraft was terrific – we were both sweating profusely. Near Aalborg, the Fw 190 pulled up into a steep climb. We followed, firing a short burst from a few hundred yards. There were flashes on the rear part of the enemy's fuselage and pieces of the tailplane fell away. The Fw 190 flicked over in a stall, diving towards us, flashed quickly past us in a steep dive, and as I started to turn, "Sticks" jubilantly called, "He's dived into the mud of the river, Bob".'

This was Braham's 29th, and final, victory. However, as they crossed the Danish coast on their way home their Mosquito was badly hit by flak, and they eventually ditched about 70 miles off the coast of Norfolk. They were fortunate to be picked up by a minesweeper, although Braham was then grounded until the invasion.

The D-Day landings saw a maximum effort being focused over the Normandy beachhead, but *Rangers* soon began to feature once more. On 16 June Sqn Ldr Herrick, with Flg Off Turski, flew one, but as the No 305 Sqn records state, 'This aircraft took off from West Raynham and

No 613 Sqn at Lasham formed part of No 138 Wing, and numbered several notable pilots amongst is crews, including Flt Lt Peter Cobley who flew Mosquito FB VI LR358/SY-O during March 1944. Cobley, who had claimed a number of successes flying Beaufighter ICs with No 242 Sqn from Malta in late 1942, did not add to his tally with the Mosquito, however. Delivered new to No 613 Sqn in late 1943, LR358 was lost in combat near Creil on 11 May 1944
(No 613 Sqn Association)

nothing more was heard of them'. In company with Wg Cdr Braham, they again headed for Aalborg, where they were intercepted by an Fw 190 from JG 1 flown by the *experte* Leutnant Robert Spreckels. The latter made short work of Herrick's Mosquito, which crashed with the loss of the crew.

Spreckels was also to prove Braham's nemesis nine days later, when the latter was shot down and made a PoW during another trip to Aalborg. His nine victories flying intruder Mosquitoes when added to his previous 20 on Blenheim and Beaufighter nightfighters made him the RAF's leading two-seat fighter pilot of the war.

COASTAL FIGHTERS

In May 1943 the Norwegian-manned, and newly formed, No 333 Sqn at Leuchars became the first unit in Coastal Command to begin re-equipping with Mosquito NF IIs, its 'B' Flight beginning operations on the 27th. The flight's primary role was the reconnaissance of the coastal waters off Norway, and its first air combat success came on 13 June 1943 when Lt Skavhaugen shot down a Do 24T-1 flying boat of *Führerkurierstaffel* Todt near Haugesund.

During July the flight claimed two 'Ju 88s' shot down, with the one credited to Finn Eriksrud on the 9th actually being a Fw 58 Weihe attached to I./JG 5 for air search and rescue duties. Eriksrud was to be one of the most successful pilots to serve with the Norwegian unit, claiming three kills by the time he became a PoW on 18 December 1943 – his Mosquito was hit by debris from his last victory (another Fw 58, downed near Bomlo), forcing him to ditch.

A bottleneck in the training of crews to fly Coastal Command Mosquitoes in the autumn of 1943 saw No 333 Sqn struggling to find attrition replacements. As a result of this shortage, experienced instructor and successful 'coastal' fighter pilot Sqn Ldr George Melville-Jackson was temporarily assigned to the unit in October. He flew his first sortie with Sgt Harald Jensen, who would himself later claim three victories as a pilot. The first of these came on 10 December when, with navigator Sub Lt Torkildsen, he caught a Ju 88D reconnaissance aircraft of 1(F)./AufklGr 120 and shot it down.

Another successful team was Sub Lts Wyller and Benjamensen, who, on 16 December off Molde, had a fight with Fw 190As of 12./JG 5 and

The first Mosquito NF II fighters issued to Coastal Command went to 'B' Flight of the Norwegian-manned No 333 Sqn at Leuchars. One of the first was DZ700/H, which was flown by several of the unit's leading pilots, and also by Sqn Ldr George Melville-Jackson, who briefly assisted with the conversion of pilots onto the Mosquito in the autumn of 1943. A long-lived aircraft which was first delivered to No 235 Sqn in early 1943, DZ700 subsequently served with four other frontline squadrons, as well as two operational training units, prior to being grounded for use as a maintenance airframe in March 1946 (*Kjetil Kornes*)

No 333 Sqn's fifth Mosquito victim was Ju 88D-1 D7+BH of *Westa* 1, flown by Unteroffizier Magnus Mannell, who was lost with his crew when they were shot down off Stavanger on 22 November 1943 by Sub Lt Finn Eriksrud. This aircraft was his second of three victories (*Kjetl Korsnes*)

Flt Lts Noel Russell (right) and Tom Armstrong (left) were one of No 235 Sqn's most successful crews. They succeeded in shooting down two Bf 109Gs off Flekkefjord on 11 January 1945 (*T Armstrong*)

downed the fighter flown by Unteroffizier Willi Surrh. Sadly, this promising crew were themselves killed in action on 23 February 1944.

Further south, on 10 March 1944 Portreath-based No 248 Sqn experienced its first major combat since swapping its Beaufighter Xs for Mosquito FB VIs and XVIIIs 'Tsetses' (fitted with a 57 mm gun). The latter, escorted by four FB VIs, attacked a U-boat that was being protected by eight Ju 88Cs. One of the Luftwaffe aircraft fell to the FB XVIII flown by Sqn Ldr Tony Phillips, who used the 57 mm cannon to great effect against the Ju 88. He also attacked the U-boat, claiming to have damaged it. Phillips was awarded the DSO later in the month, and was given command of the squadron soon afterwards.

On 27 March No 248 Sqn was joined by Beaufighter X-equipped No 235 Sqn at Portreath, and two months later the unit also received FB VIs. The two units then combined to form the first all-Mosquito strike wing to work over Biscay. Serving with No 235 Sqn at the time was Flg Off Noel Russell, who already had several claims to his credit following a tour with No 272 Sqn flying Beaufighters in North Africa in 1942-43.

On D-Day No 248 Sqn was one of the RAF's busiest Mosquito units, and the following day Wg Cdr Tony Phillips shot down an Fw 190 – sadly, he was killed in action on 4 July.

Both squadrons had regular contact with the Luftwaffe over Biscay during the summer of 1944, before they moved north to Banff in September to join the Norwegians of 'B' Flight, No 333 Sqn. The Banff Wing was commanded by the ebullient Gp Capt Max Aitken, a highly capable pilot who had no fewer than 14 and one shared victories to his credit flying Hurricanes, Spitfires

Mosquito FB VI HR118/3-W of No 235 Sqn, flown by Flg Off Noel Russell, is seen here escorting frigates on 18 July 1944 whilst the unit was based at Portreath, in Cornwall (*T Armstrong*)

and Beaufighters. Despite having flown these RAF greats in combat since 1940, he recorded that 'the Mosquito was a sensation!'

The wing's first Mosquito victory was credited to Wt Off Charles Cogswell on 24 October, when he destroyed a Bf 110 during a strike off Bergen (he also got a Ju 88 on 21 April 1945). Minutes later Flt Lt Arthur Jacques shot down two Messerschmitt fighters – he was to claim a third over Sogne Fjord on the 30th to take his tally to three, which was no mean achievement for a strike pilot.

One of the biggest engagements between the Banff Wing and the Luftwaffe came on 11 January 1945 during an anti-shipping strike to Flekkefjord flown by four aircraft from No 235 Sqn and six from No 248 Sqn. The Mosquitoes were attacked by a formation of fighters, and in the subsequent combat three Bf 109s were shot down, two falling to Noel Russell. The squadron's operational diary recorded;

'Flt Lt Russell attacked one Me 109 from dead astern, range 300 down to 50 yards, scoring strikes. The enemy aircraft, seen to be on fire, hit the sea and exploded. They then attacked one of a pair of Me 109s from 300 down to 100 yards, again scoring strikes, and this aircraft too was seen to hit the sea.'

In all, the Mosquito crews claimed three Bf 109s and an Fw 190 destroyed, as well as a second Focke-Wulf fighter as a probable and a third damaged.

The Mosquito units continued to take a heavy toll of enemy shipping, with little sign of the Luftwaffe, through to the third week of April 1945. The last big encounter came during a U-boat hunt on the 21st of that month when, over the Kattegat, no fewer than eight Ju 88s fell to Mosquitoes. A frustrated Sqn Ldr Herbert Gunnis (a five-kill Beaufighter ace with No 252 Sqn in North Africa) of No 248 Sqn recalled 'the sea was full of blazing aircraft. Five times I got a Ju in my sights and each time another Mosquito crew shot it down before I could draw a bead!'

No 235 Sqn was also successful, with Wt Off Cogswell shooting down a Ju 88 and damaging a Ju 188 (his last claims), while Heine Eriksen of No 333 Sqn also shot a Ju 88 down to claim his unit's 18th, and final, aerial victory.

COLOUR PLATES

1
Mosquito NF II DD673/YP-E of Sqn Ldr N J Starr, No 23 Sqn, Manston, 23 August 1942

2
Mosquito FB VI HJ675/YP-V of Flt Lt P W Rabone, No 23 Sqn, Luqa, Malta, 8 July 1943

3
Mosquito NF XXX MT487/ZK-L of Flt Lt D H Greaves, No 25 Sqn, Castle Camps, October 1944

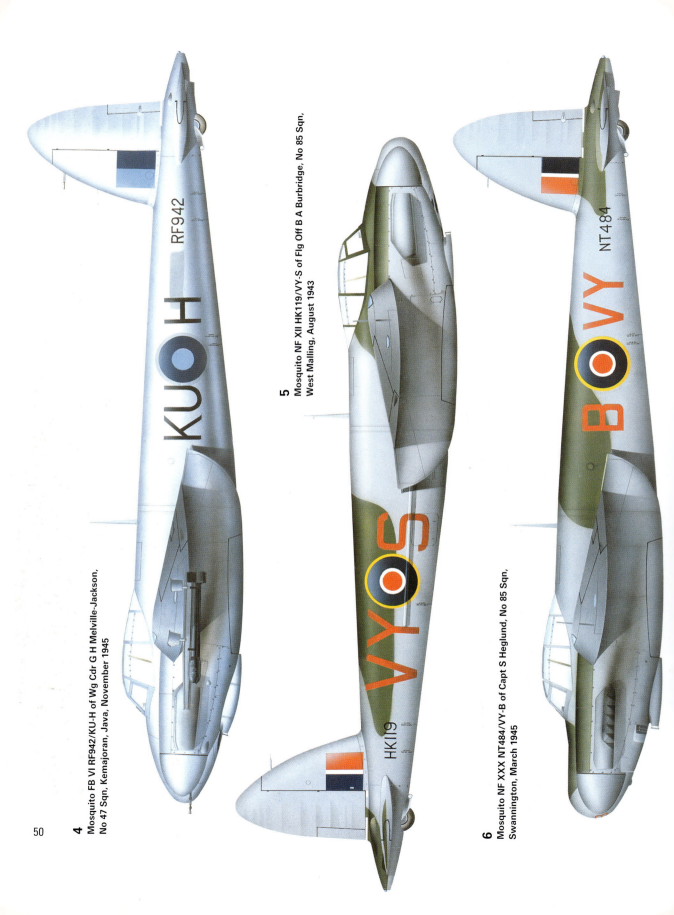

4
Mosquito FB VI RF942/KU-H of Wg Cdr G H Melville-Jackson,
No 47 Sqn, Kemajoran, Java, November 1945

5
Mosquito NF XII HK119/VY-S of Flg Off B A Burbridge, No 85 Sqn,
West Malling, August 1943

6
Mosquito NF XXX NT484/VY-B of Capt S Heglund, No 85 Sqn,
Swannington, March 1945

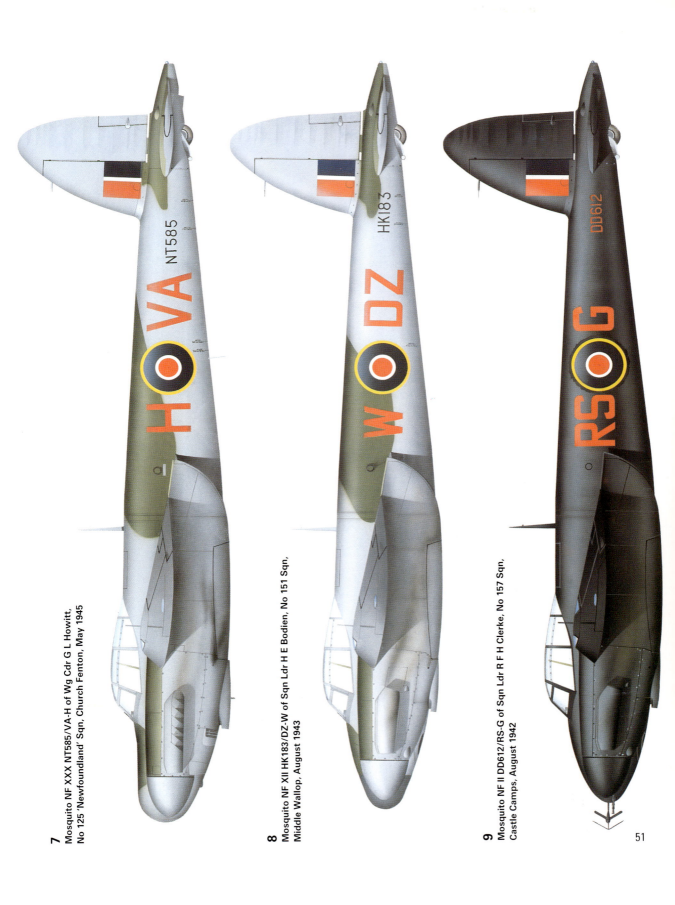

7
Mosquito NF XXX NT585/VA-H of Wg Cdr G L Howitt, No 125 'Newfoundland' Sqn, Church Fenton, May 1945

8
Mosquito NF XII HK183/DZ-W of Sqn Ldr H E Bodien, No 151 Sqn, Middle Wallop, August 1943

9
Mosquito NF II DD612/RS-G of Sqn Ldr R F H Clerke, No 157 Sqn, Castle Camps, August 1942

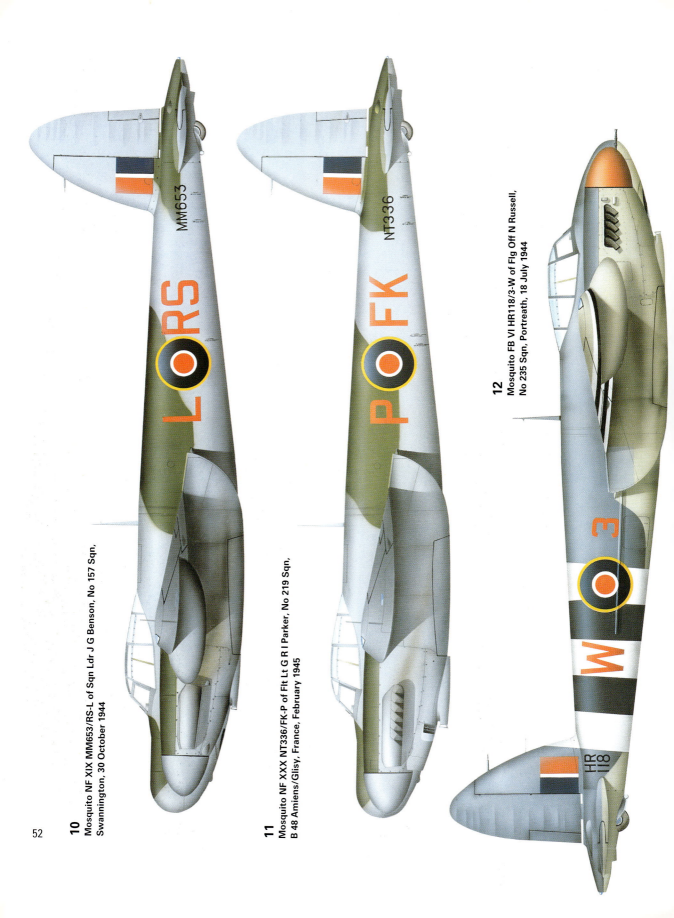

10
Mosquito NF XIX MM653/RS-L of Sqn Ldr J G Benson, No 157 Sqn, Swannington, 30 October 1944

11
Mosquito NF XXX NT336/FK-P of Flt Lt G R I Parker, No 219 Sqn, B 48 Amiens/Glisy, France, February 1945

12
Mosquito FB VI HR118/3-W of Flg Off N Russell, No 235 Sqn, Portreath, 18 July 1944

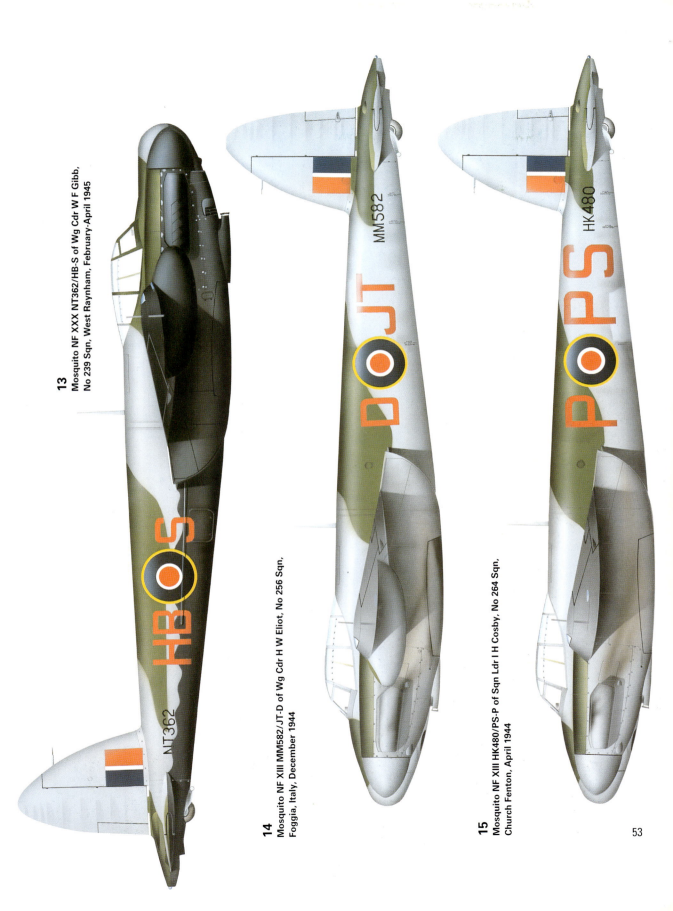

13
Mosquito NF XXX NT362/HB-S of Wg Cdr W F Gibb, No 239 Sqn, West Raynham, February-April 1945

14
Mosquito NF XIII MM582/JT-D of Wg Cdr H W Eliot, No 256 Sqn, Foggia, Italy, December 1944

15
Mosquito NF XIII HK480/PS-P of Sqn Ldr I H Cosby, No 264 Sqn, Church Fenton, April 1944

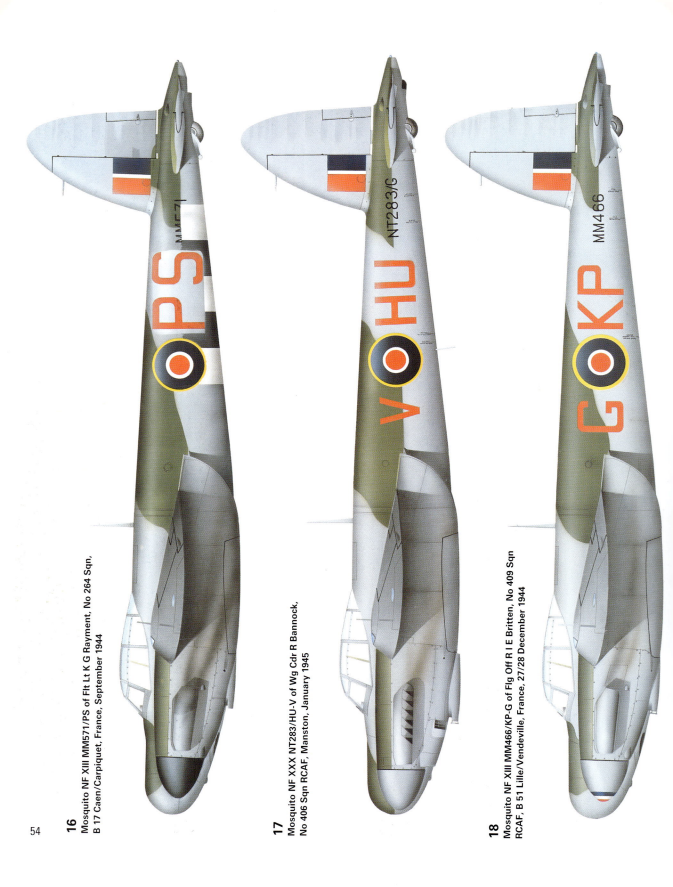

16
Mosquito NF XIII MM571/PS of Flt Lt K G Rayment, No 264 Sqn, B 17 Caen/Carpiquet, France, September 1944

17
Mosquito NF XXX NT283/HU-V of Wg Cdr R Bannock, No 406 Sqn RCAF, Manston, January 1945

18
Mosquito NF XIII MM466/KP-G of Flg Off R I E Britten, No 409 Sqn RCAF, B 51 Lille/Vendeville, France, 27/28 December 1944

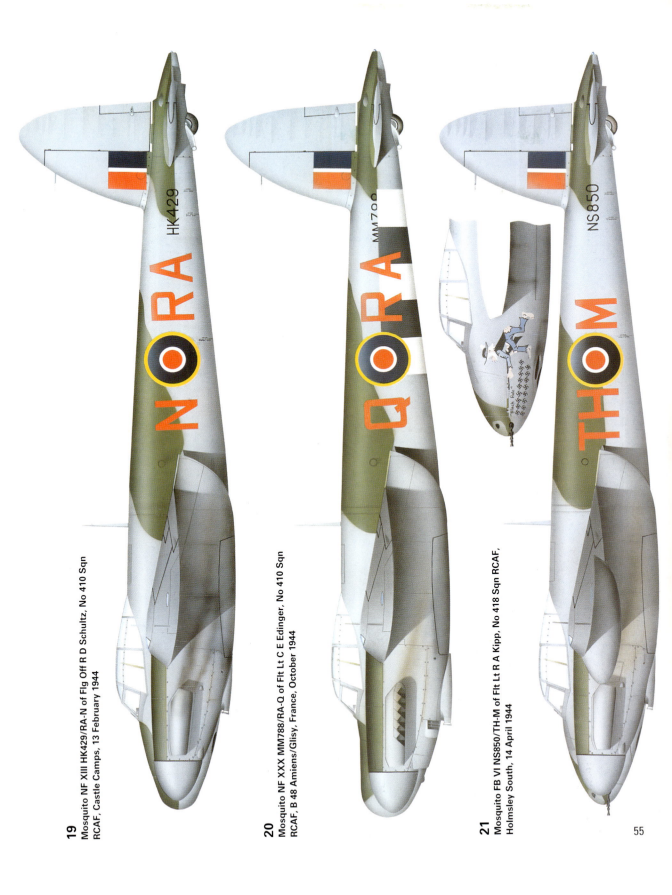

19
Mosquito NF XIII HK429/RA-N of Flg Off R D Schultz, No 410 Sqn RCAF, Castle Camps, 13 February 1944

20
Mosquito NF XXX MM788/RA-Q of Flt Lt C E Edinger, No 410 Sqn RCAF, B 48 Amiens/Glisy, France, October 1944

21
Mosquito FB VI NS850/TH-M of Flt Lt R A Kipp, No 418 Sqn RCAF, Holmsley South, 14 April 1944

22
Mosquito NF XXX NT311/RX-L of Sqn Ldr R B Cowper, No 456 Sqn RAAF, Bradwell Bay, March 1945

23
Mosquito FB VI MM417/EG-T of Wg Cdr I S Smith, No 487 Sqn RNZAF, Hunsdon, March 1944

24
Mosquito NF XIII MM466/ME-R of Flt Lt G E Jameson, No 488 Sqn RNZAF, Colerne, 29/30 July 1944

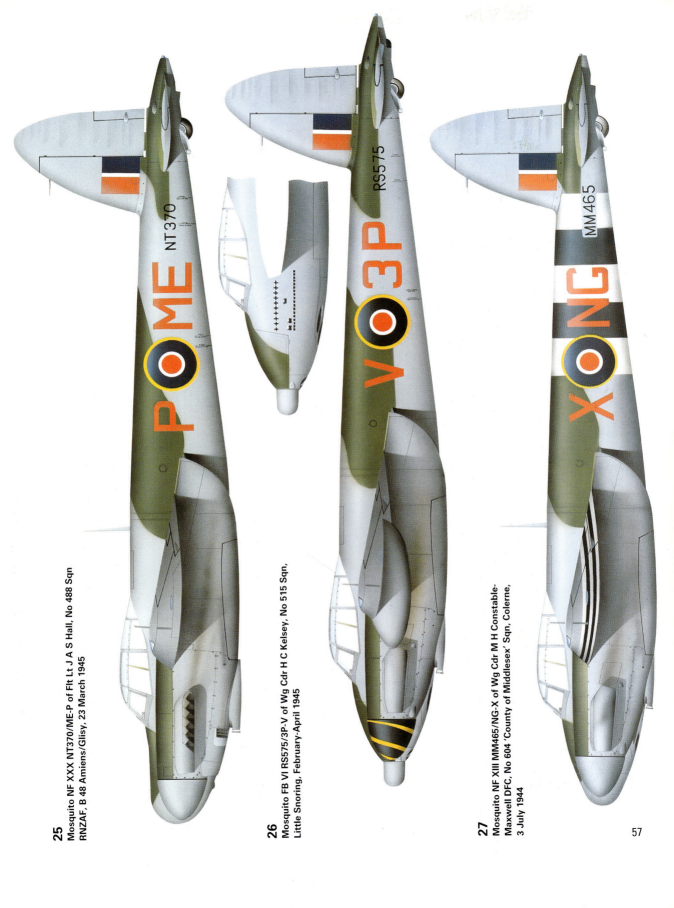

25
Mosquito NF XXX NT370/ME-P of Flt Lt J A S Hall, No 488 Sqn RNZAF, B 48 Amiens/Glisy, 23 March 1945

26
Mosquito FB VI RS575/3P-V of Wg Cdr H C Kelsey, No 515 Sqn, Little Snoring, February-April 1945

27
Mosquito NF XIII MM465/NG-X of Wg Cdr M H Constable-Maxwell DFC, No 604 'County of Middlesex' Sqn, Colerne, 3 July 1944

28
Mosquito NF XIII MM552/NG-N of Flt Lt R J Foster, No 604 'County of Middlesex' Sqn, Colerne, 3/4 August 1944

29
Mosquito NF II DZ716/UP-L of Wg Cdr G Denholm, No 605 'County of Warwick' Sqn, Ford, March 1943

30
Mosquito FB VI NS838/UP-J of Flt Lt A D Wagner, No 605 'County of Warwick' Sqn, Bradwell Bay, 5 March 1944

NEMESIS OF THE NACHTJAGD

The performance of the Mosquito made it a natural selection for the intruder role thanks to its range, speed and firepower. In mid-1942 No 23 Sqn, led by its ebullient 30-year-old CO, Wg Cdr B R O 'Bertie' Hoare, began replacing its Havoc Is and Boston IIs with all-black Mosquito NF IIs. Hoare, who already had three victories from his time flying Blenheim IFs and Havoc Is with No 23 Sqn in 1941-42, flew the unit's first NF II intruder to Caen on the night of 5 July. The following night he flew NF II DD670/YP-S on another patrol over central France, with Wt Off J F Potter as navigator, as described in the unit's records;

'When east of Chartres, they saw in the distance an enemy aircraft with navigation lights on. The aircraft was stalked, and after three short bursts of cannon fire it caught fire and crashed near Montdidier.'

They had shot down a Do 217 – the first of many victims for the Mosquito in the enemy's backyard. Three weeks later Hoare, who was awarded the DSO for his leadership of No 23 Sqn, flew his 80th, and final, trip as CO before he handed command of the unit over to Wg Cdr Peter Wykeham-Barnes, who was himself an ace from the fighting in the Western Desert. Wykeham-Barnes began operational flying in mid-

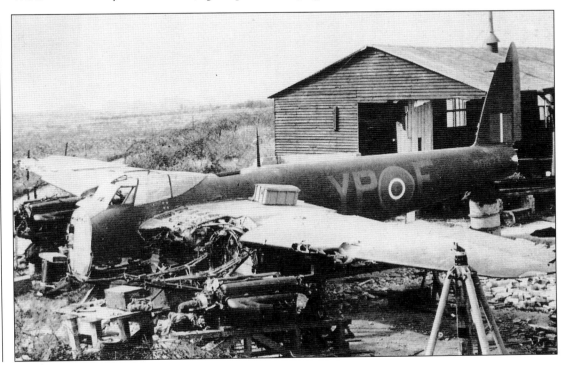

On the night of 23 August 1942, all-black Mosquito NF II DD673/YP-E of No 23 Sqn, flown by future five-kill ace Sqn Ldr N J Starr, set off from Manston for Deelen. However, ten miles off the Dutch coast, the aircraft's port engine failed and Starr was forced to return home. Landing at high speed, the fighter went off the end of the runway and collided with a steamroller. As the squadron records subsequently recorded, 'it lost the engagement!' *(Michael Bowyer)*

CHAPTER FOUR

Battle of Britain ace Wg Cdr George Denholm, who had a total of six victories, three of which were shared, was CO of No 605 Sqn when it replaced its Havoc I/IIs with Mosquito NF IIs in early 1943 (*David Ross*)

October. Hoare went on to claim three more aerial victories whilst leading FB VI-equipped No 605 Sqn in 1943-44.

Although the aerial defence of the UK remained the priority, No 23 Sqn's intruders also played an important part in blunting the Luftwaffe's bombing offensive on southern England. However, after five successful months of intruder operations, during the afternoon of 6 December 1942 the unit was unexpectedly withdrawn from operations. After receiving new aircraft it made ready to depart overseas for Malta, and crews began flying the Mosquitoes out from Portreath just before Christmas.

In February 1943 Ford-based No 605 Sqn, under the command of pre-war Auxiliary pilot Wg Cdr George Denholm (who had also 'made ace' flying Spitfires with No 603 Sqn in 1940), began replacing its Havoc IIs and Boston IIIs with Mosquito NF IIs. Denholm, with Sgt Ray as his navigator, flew No 605 Sqn's first Mosquito operation on 10 March, and the following night they sortied up to Holland. Over the Luftwaffe base at Gilze-Rijen, the crew attacked and damaged an unidentified aircraft, opening the squadron's Mosquito account. Two days later No 605 Sqn moved to Castle Camps, in Cambridgeshire.

March 1943 also saw the RCAF intruder unit No 418 Sqn at Ford replace its Boston IIIs with Mosquito NF IIs. Bomb-carrying FB VIs arrived two months later, and the unit was fully equipped with the fighter-bomber variant by July. Its fortunes then rapidly improved, such that by the end of hostilities No 418 Sqn would count nine aces among its members.

FLOWER AND MAHMOUD

During June No 605 Sqn began flying bomber support *Flower* patrols against enemy nightfighter bases, and on the night of 17/18 August

George Denholm flew No 605 Sqn's first Mosquito operation, and on 11 March 1943, in this aircraft (DZ716/UP-L), he also made its first claim with the type when he probably destroyed an unidentified German aircraft during an intruder to the Dutch airfield at Gilze-Rijen. This proved to be Denholm's final claim (*David Ross*)

ex-Battle of Britain Hurricane pilot Flt Lt David Blomely, and his navigator Flg Off Birrell, flew FB VI HJ808/UP-O in support of the bombing raid on the secret enemy rocket establishment at Peenemunde. They were attacked by a *Wilde Sau* Bf 109G east of Schleswig, which overshot the Mosquito and was promptly shot down into the sea, where its tail could be seen sticking out of the water.

On 21 September Blomely, again in HJ808/UP-O, shot down two Ju 88s in daylight west of the Skaggerak, and he followed this up on 9 November with a Bf 110 west of Aalborg. Blomely's four Intruder kills (all in HJ808) combined with his solitary May 1940 Hurricane victory with No 151 Sqn over Dunkirk to make him an ace.

Intruding was a hazardous business, however, and this was brutally brought home to No 605 Sqn on the night of 22/23 September. Flg Off K F 'Dizzy' Dacre, who appeared destined to become the unit's next ace having scored four confirmed victories and two damaged between 19 June and 15 September, was lost with his navigator, Sgt S R Didsbury, intruding in the Hannover area in FB VI HJ790/UP-R.

Later that same month Wg Cdr 'Sammy' Hoare returned to operations as No 605 Sqn's CO, and on the night of 27/28 September he shot down a Do 217 on his first mission (in FB VI UP-L). That same day another formidable character joined his squadron in the person of Rhodesian Flg Off Leo Williams. Having two Mosquito victories from a previous tour with No 23 Sqn, he would claim a further five kills with the unit in 1944 to 'make ace'. In October 1943 No 605 Sqn welcomed Flt Lt Alan Wagner, who had three victories to his credit, including two Japanese 'Val' dive-bombers downed over Ceylon whilst flying Hurricanes with No 30 Sqn in 1942 – his first kill came in a No 151 Sqn Defiant in 1941. He was crewed at No 605 Sqn with Flg Off 'Pip' Orringe.

October 1943 also saw 'A' Flight of No 25 Sqn begin fitting AI Mk IV radar to its NF IIs for *Mahmoud* bomber support sorties, where the Mosquito crews hunted enemy nightfighters.

On 18 November the Battle of Berlin began, and at Ford the Fighter Interception Unit (FIU) had been examining the problems of supporting the bomber streams over Germany. The specialist unit's CO was seven-victory ace Wg Cdr Rory Chisholm, and that night, with navigator Flt Lt Frank Clarke (who was to be killed in action a week later), he sortied to Mannheim in NF II HJ705 which had been fitted with tail warning

From March 1943, the Mosquito FB VIs of No 418 Sqn wreaked widespread havoc on the enemy during a series of highly successful intruder operations that also resulted in the creation of no fewer than nine aces. This particular FB VI was one of the last examples delivered to No 418 Sqn, being taken on strength in early 1945. It subsequently served with No 69 Sqn post-war and was eventually struck off charge in August 1947 (*author's collection*)

radar. Eventually arriving over the blazing city, the crew eerily spotted a number of bombers in the gloom before Clarke gained a contact. Chisholm recalled what happened next in his autobiography, *Cover of Darkness*;

'I turned as hard as I could. Our radar showed that he was after us, and initially I thought only of saving my skin. I was trying to outmanoeuvre him so as to come up from behind, where his radar was blind. And on we went, milling round with our invisible opponent.'

Clarke soon called 'He's ahead now, I think. Stop turning. Steady. That's fine, he's 2000 ft away'. Chisholm continued;

'"That's it, have a look. It's a 110. You must watch this. By now we had closed right up and fell back slowly as we came up level. I opened fire from about a hundred yards, and hits registered immediately on that luckless aircraft – there was a vivid flash and I had to pause to take aim again. I fired, and there were more flashes – my windscreen became momentarily obscured by some liquid as he turned and dived away. I saw against the blackness of the ground what might have been a Catherine wheel close to us, but a moment later it hit the ground and exploded.'

Chisholm, having claimed his ninth, and final, victory, then headed for home. He was later promoted and rewarded with a staff job at HQ No 100 Group, which was formed just a few days later. The group controlled a mixture of offensive nightfighter and electronic jamming squadrons whose job it was to provide bomber support in an effort to reduce the escalating losses of four-engined 'heavies' over Germany.

No 141 Sqn, which was just re-equipping with 'Serrate' homer-fitted Mosquito NF IIs in place of its Beaufighter VIFs, was the first fighter squadron to join the group. It was followed by a reformed No 239 Sqn, and they were both based at West Raynham. Nos 515 and 169 Sqns, at Little Snoring, were also reassigned to No 100 Group at this time. The latter was commanded by ex-Battle of Britain and Malta Hurricane and Spitfire ace Wg Cdr E J 'Jumbo' Gracie, who was described by a contemporary as 'a little fire eater'!

In spite of Mosquito serviceability problems, No 141 Sqn flew No 100 Group's first offensive nightfighter mission in support of a Main Force raid on Berlin on 16 December. 'Jumbo' Gracie performed his squadron's first operation to the Hamburg area in mid January 1944, covering a Berlin raid, but without success. That distinction went to Sqn Ldr Joe Cooper on 30 January when he shot down Oberleutnant Loeffelmaan's Bf 110G, D5+LB of *Stab* III./NJG 3 just east of Berlin. Forty-eight hours earlier, Flg Offs Harry White and Mike Allan of No 141 Sqn (in NF II HJ941/TW-X) had claimed No 100 Group's first Mosquito victory when they shot down a Bf 109 *Wilde Sau* fighter near Berlin for their fourth of an eventual twelve victories.

No hiding place

The Mosquito intruder units had also been kept busy in late 1943/early 1944, and on 12 December future ten-kill FB VI ace Flt Lt Robert Kipp of No 418 Sqn claimed his first victory when he shared in the destruction of an He 111 near Bourges and probably destroyed another. On the night of 10 January 1944 'Sammy' Hoare destroyed a Ju 188 near Chievres for No 605 Sqn's 100th victory.

During the afternoon of 27 January two No 418 Sqn FB VIs flown by future aces Flt Lt Jim Johnson and Flg Off John Caine carried out a Day *Ranger* to central France. As they approached Bourges at low level, they found a hapless W 34 light transport aircraft, which they literally blew apart with their combined fire. Continuing south, they separated near Clermont Ferrand and Johnson damaged a Ju 86 as it came in to land. He then pulled up and saw further aircraft. Selecting a Ju 88 flying at 1500 ft, he closed in and fired to a distance 100 yards, sending it down. John Caine also found a Ju 88, whose fate he later grimly described;

'He started to fall in pieces and the port motor fell off. The whole left side of the cockpit sheared off, and we saw the pilot slumped forward over the instrument panel. Immediately afterwards, one of the crew came rolling out and later we saw him floating down with his parachute open.'

Rejoining, the pair then found another W 34, which also fell to their guns before they turned for home and a night landing, Jim Johnson having become No 418 Sqn's first ace during the course of this highly eventful sortie.

Their CO, Wg Cdr D C S MacDonald, and his wingman Australian Flt Lt Charles Scherf, were also over France on the afternoon of 27 January. As they approached Bourges the CO shot down an He 111, while to the southeast Scherf came up behind a luckless Fw 200 Condor and fired a ten-second burst into it. The aircraft was sent cart-wheeling into a wood for the first of the Australian's 13 and one shared victories.

Standing in front of FB VI *MOONBEAM McSWINE* on 3 April 1944 are two of No 418 Sqn's outstanding intruder crews. They are, from left to right, Sqn Ldr Howie Cleveland, Flt Sgt Frank Day, Lt James Luma (USAAF on secondment) and Flg Off Colin Finlayson. Both Cleveland and Luma (who regularly flew this aircraft) had recently become aces when this photograph was taken, Luma's big day coming on 21 March 1944 when, during an attack on Luxeuil, he shot down two enemy aircraft, destroyed two more on the ground and damaged four more! (*Canadian Forces*)

The CO also brought down an He 177 in an outstanding day's work for the Canadian squadron, which then began a run of great success.

On 13 February American 1Lt James Luma, who was serving with No 418 Sqn in order to gain nightfighting experience, and his navigator, Flg Off Colin Finlayson, flew to the Bordeaux area in search of long-range bombers that were harassing Atlantic convoys. Luma, who in March would duly become the first USAAF pilot to 'make ace' flying the Mosquito, described how he spotted the lights of an aircraft (an He 177) near an airfield at 0200 hrs;

'We gave him a two-second burst 150 yards from below and astern. There was an explosion in the region of the cockpit, and as we shot under him, he appeared to be diving down after us. He went straight in three miles south of Bordeaux.'

Several nights later, on 18/19 February, Robert Kipp conducted what was described as a classic intruder sortie on the night that 200 enemy bombers attacked London. He caught two Me 410s as they returned to their Juvincourt base, in France, shooting both of them down.

On 24 February No 418 Sqn's Flt Lt Don MacFadyen, who was described as being 'an able pilot, though he was a compulsive perfectionist, appallingly egocentric', flew a five-and-a-half-hour mission to southern Germany. Approaching Wurzburg airfield in FB VI NS830/TH-G, he spotted an Me 410 and coolly flew around the circuit with the aircraft, before sending it down into a river for the first of his seven victories. The next night No 418 Sqn despatched aircraft on *Flower* patrols, one of which was flown by Flg Off John Caine and Wt Off Earl Boal, who strafed and blew up a taxiing Bf 110 at Munich-Reim airfield before it could take off.

Later that afternoon No 418 Sqn's Charles Scherf and future ace Sqn Ldr Howie Cleveland set out on what would become an epic Day *Ranger* to central France. Initially destroying several aircraft on the ground at St Yan, the two Mosquito pilots spotted a bizarre-looking He 111Z twin-fuselage glider tug towing two Gotha Go 242 gliders at 2000 ft near Dole airfield a short while later. The pair went straight for them, Cleveland opening fire first and almost colliding with the rear glider as the tow parted and it pitched up and crashed.

Scherf duly went after the second glider, and it too disintegrated under his burst of cannon fire – his fifth victory – before the pair then attacked the Heinkel that the Australian later described as 'the Monstrosity'. His fire set the starboard engine ablaze, and Cleveland then hit the starboard side before Scherf made another firing pass. With three of its five engines on fire,

The nose of No 605 Sqn's FB VI NS838 *WAG'S "WAR-WAGON"* includes two Japanese symbols for the victories its pilot, Flg Off Alan Wagner (left), claimed over Ceylon in April 1942. He became an ace in this aircraft on 5 March 1944 when flying with his navigator, Flg Off 'Pip' Orringe (right) (*Ian Piper*)

and shedding wreckage, the He 111 slowly spiralled into the ground. Slightly tongue in cheek, No 418 Sqn tried to claim two victories for the ungainly Heinkel as it had two fuselages! This sortie was Scherf's last operation of his tour, but like so many others, he occasionally returned to his old unit to 'guest', and over the next three months he more than doubled his score.

No 605 Sqn also remained busy during this period, and over Germany on 5 March Alan Wagner and 'Pip' Orringe, in FB VI *WAG'S "WAR-WAGON"*, had a field-day as a contemporary press report described;

'Flying over clearly lit bases on the Continent, two aircraft of the same squadron shot down four enemy aircraft. Three of these fell to Flt Lt A D Wagner DFC of Croydon. Earlier today he said, "I chased another one and hit him with our last ammunition, but our windscreen was covered with oil from one of the three we had destroyed and so we could not assess the damage". One of Flt Lt Wagner's victims blew up when he closed to less than 50 yards before opening fire.'

Wagner had destroyed an Fw 190 over Gardelegen airfield, which gave him ace status, before shooting down two Me 410s and then damaging a third, as described above.

Bomber Crisis

Through the winter the nightfighter units of No 100 Group also began to improve their tactics and training, and it was hoped that they would soon be able to help reduce the increasingly serious losses being suffered by the Bomber Command Main Force. However, they claimed only four victories in February 1944, one of which (an He 177 *bomber*, claimed on the night of the 15th) fell to No 141 Sqn's Flg Offs Harry White and Mike Allan, who were destined to become the group's most successful crew. This victory, near Berlin, took their tally to five. White, who was in DZ726/TW-Z, described his 'ace-making' action thus;

'Throttling back and turning hard starboard then hard port until AI contact was regained, I then closed gently to dead astern and gave a three-second burst of cannon. This resulted in a fire in the fuselage and starboard engine. The aircraft turned gently to starboard and I gave another burst and the fires increased until the aircraft, which was now clearly seen to be an He 177, went spiralling down into the cloud, enveloped in flames.'

However, in spite of the presence of the Mosquito nightfighters, no fewer than 43 bombers were lost that night, followed by a staggering 78 during a raid on Leipzig 72 hours later.

One week later, on 24/25 February, No 169 Sqn's Flt Lt Tim Woodman (in NF II DZ254) spotted a Bf 110 over Mannheim silhouetted against the snow-covered landscape below, and he hit its port engine and wing, sending the first of his seven victims down – his Mosquito was struck by debris and damaged during the engagement. However, tempering his success was the loss of his CO, 'Jumbo' Gracie, near Hannover, which dealt a severe blow to the unit.

The so-called Battle of Berlin ended on 24 March, having cost the Allies no fewer than 625 bombers destroyed. The Mosquito nightfighters also suffered losses too, with No 239 Sqn having a crew shot down on this raid, adding to two more posted missing in the previous week. Then on

One of No 151 Sqn's most successful crews consisted of the unit CO, Wg Cdr Geoffrey Goodman (left), and Flg Off W F Thomas (right) who, during the spring of 1944, shot down eight German aircraft. Six of their kills came during intruder missions over France, including four He 111s shot down in an incredible daytime sortie on 4 May (*WW2images.com*)

the night of the 30th came the Nuremburg raid, when some 95 RAF bombers were lost and the Mosquitoes claimed just a solitary Bf 110 in return. In the wake of this unmitigated disaster, RAF High Command decided to allocate two additional Mosquito nightfighter squadrons to No 100 Group for bomber support, and on 1 May the experienced Nos 85 and 157 Sqns were transferred to Swannington, in Norfolk.

The number of victories falling to the bomber support nightfighters did increase significantly through the spring, however, with claims for 15 destroyed in April and 16 in May – most of these fell to No 239 Sqn. Yet, the outstanding individual effort during this period was by No 169 Sqn crew Plt Offs W H 'Andy' Miller and Freddie Bone who, on 15/16 May, shot down a Bf 110 and two Ju 88s in the Cuxhaven area when supporting a mining operation in NF II DZ748. The 22-year-old Welshman's fifth victory (of eleven kills) had come three weeks earlier when, during a raid on Cologne, he had shot down a Bf 110.

In spite of these efforts, 37 bombers were lost on 15/16 May, as 'Andy' Miller wistfully recalled;

'It was a moonlit night, and when we did spot the Germans they were everywhere, but it was too late. You could follow the path of the bombers using the flaming wrecks on the ground. As I became more experienced I could anticipate when and where the German nightfighters would attack by plotting which beacon they would assemble over.'

Two victories went to Flt Lt Dennis Hughes of No 239 Sqn late in the month, while on the night of 31 May his colleagues Flt Lt Dennis Welfare and Flg Off 'Taff' Bellis (in NF II DZ256/HB-U) engaged a Bf 110 near Trappes, as the latter recalled;

'We picked up a Serrate transmission north of Paris. We then manoeuvred our "Mossie" to get behind the transmitting aircraft. To our dismay, it switched off its radar before we were in AI contact. However, we kept on the same course and picked up on an AI contact a minute or so later. We converted this to a visual and shot down an Me 110.'

It was No 239 Sqn's tenth victory during the month.

May had also seen the Luftwaffe begin to introduce the SN-2 radar which the Serrate receivers fitted into the NF IIs could not pick up. Once widely introduced, the new radar nullified many of No 100 Group's tactics, and later in the summer the number of kills dropped markedly.

The intruders too continued to play their part, with some nightfighters from ADGB units also undertaking these sorties to the west. One such mission was made to the Dijon area on 4 May by No 151 Sqn's CO, Wg Cdr Geoffrey Goodman (in NF XIII MM446/DZ-Q), who had become an ace the previous month;

'About eight miles west of the town we sighted three aircraft flying in vic formation, travelling in an easterly direction – the aircraft were

Mosquito FB VI HR250/DZ-P of No 151 Sqn is seen at Predannack between missions in the summer of 1944, when the squadron was kept busy flying over Biscay and western France. The crewmen standing in front of the aircraft are thought to be seconded Royal New Zealand Navy Volunteer Reserve officers Lts Cramp and Maggs, who, on the morning of 15 August, shot down a Do 24 near Chalons and damaged a Bf 109. Delivered new to No 151 Sqn, HR250 later served with No 29 Sqn. Post-war, it spent time with the Central Fighter Establishment and No 1 Overseas Ferry Unit, before eventually being sold to the Yugoslav Air Force in January 1952 (*M N Austin*)

identified as He 111s. The starboard aircraft was straggling in the formation, and we climbed underneath him and I fired two bursts. It caught fire and then fell to starboard in a steep dive, burning hard.'

They then attacked the other two He 111s and sent them down. Goodman continued;

'At this point I noticed we were right over the aerodrome, and that a fourth aircraft was making a wide circuit. I turned in behind and gave this one a three-second burst, which set the starboard engine on fire, and it went down in a steep dive to hit the ground northwest of the aerodrome.'

Two days later Sqn Ldr Charles Cooke, who was the original Mosquito nightfighter ace, and also now with No 151 Sqn, made his final claim on a *Ranger* near Bourges;

'We turned to starboard and identified an Fw 190. I carried out an attack from astern. Strikes were seen on the port wing root, whereupon it burst into flames and the port aileron came off – a piece struck the top of the port radiator cover on my aircraft. It was then seen to turn and dive into the ground.'

On 16 May newly promoted Sqn Ldr Charles Scherf and Sqn Ldr Howie Cleveland of No 418 Sqn headed for the Kiel area on what turned out to be one of the outstanding *Ranger* sorties of the war. As the two Mosquito pilots coasted in, they spotted an He 111, and following a five-minute chase the Australian hit the bomber with a short burst from 150 yards and sent it crashing into the sea on fire. Moving on to Zingst, they spotted an Fw 190 doing practice rocket attacks. Scherf climbed from tree-top height and hauled round after the German pilot as he attempted to evade. With a superb piece of deflection shooting from 300 yards, he hit the fighter, which burst into flames, and another short burst completed the job.

The pair then headed for Parrow airfield, on the German coast, where Scherf made a head-on pass on an He 177 from slightly below his quarry's height. From 150 yards, he sent shells into the bomber's cockpit and set its engines on fire, before it too crashed into the sea. Howie Cleveland now got in on the action and attacked an He 111 as it tried to land, shooting it down – this kill made him an ace. Having blown up a second He 111 on the ground, Scherf then spotted an Hs 123 biplane and quickly shot the ground attack aircraft out of the sky.

Cleveland had also destroyed a Do 217 on the ground at Parrow, but his Mosquito had been hit by flak soon afterwards, injuring both him and his navigator, Flt Sgt F Day. He therefore headed for neutral Sweden and ditched offshore, where, by an incredible effort, Cleveland extricated the badly wounded Day. He could not get him into a dinghy, however, and by the time rescuers arrived, Day had drowned. Cleveland was repatriated a month later and returned to No 418 Sqn, making his final claim on 27 July and eventually commanding the unit.

Despite the loss of his wingman, Scherf was not yet finished. He and his navigator, Flg Off Finlayson, damaged a Do 18 at anchor, and whilst flying over Stralsund they spotted a lone Ju 86P. Although hit by some unpleasantly accurate flak whilst closing on the elderly Junkers machine, he scored hits on both engines and the Ju 86 blew up and crashed near the town. Having claimed five aircraft shot down, one destroyed on the ground and another one damaged, Scherf and Finlayson then left the devastated area. Although their flak-damaged FB VI suffered a number of bird strikes en route to their base at Coltishall, Scherf managed to land safely. This proved to be his final operational flight. Scherf was awarded a DSO soon afterwards, and at his farewell dinner, the Chief of Air Staff said 'I believe you are the most outstanding airman I have ever known'.

D-Day Record

No 605 Sqn gained a unique first for itself in the early hours of D-Day morning when it sortied 18 aircraft from its Manston base, as the squadron diary recounted;

'Flg Off Roy Lelong and Flt Sgt J A McLaren were sent to the Evreux and St Andre areas. When Evreux lit up, Roy obtained a visual on an aircraft silhouetted against the clouds, and with the help of the moon he recognised it as an Me 410. He then throttled back, pulled to dead astern and opened fire. Hits were seen around the cockpit area and the aircraft burst into flames. It then slowly lost height in a spiral dive and crashed. His victim, which was attacked at 0418 hrs, was later confirmed as being the first enemy aircraft destroyed by any unit on the morning of D-Day.'

This victory was the second of seven kills eventually credited to the 27-year-old New Zealander.

The build up to the invasion had meant that much of the heavy bomber effort had been focused on logistics targets in the Normandy area, thus reducing the number of losses suffered by Bomber Command. Nonetheless, the bomber support nightfighters were taking an

No 239 Sqn's Flt Lts Dennis Welfare and 'Taff' Bellis stand in front of their badly singed Mosquito NF II DZ256/HB-U at West Raynham on 12 June 1944 after being doused in burning petrol from a Bf 110 that they had shot down near Paris – Welfare's fifth victory. The pair claimed four aircraft destroyed whilst flying this aircraft, which had previously served with Nos 25 and 410 Sqns. Quickly repaired and returned to operational service, DZ256 was written off on 27 October 1944 when it spun into the ground near Newark whilst still assigned to No 239 Sqn (*David Bellis*)

increasing toll of the *nachtjagd*, and more crews were reaching the five-victory milestone.

On 11 June No 239 Sqn's Flt Lt Dennis Welfare and Flg Off D B Bellis added to their growing tally during a patrol near Paris. Homing in on a Serrate contact, Bellis recalled visually acquiring the target, which clearly showed the 'twin fins and exhausts of an Me 110. We attacked from 50 yards, and the Me immediately blew up. Our "Mossie" flew into the debris and was enveloped by burning petrol'. Although their fighter (NF II DZ256/HB-U) was badly damaged, the crew coaxed it back to West Raynham. Later that month, on 24/25 June, Dennis Welfare destroyed a Ju 88 again near Paris to become the RAF's newest ace.

No 100 Group's own intruders of No 515 Sqn also made claims in June, with veteran ace Sqn Ldr Paul Rabone being credited with a rare daylight kill when he downed a Bf 110 over Eelde airfield on the 22nd. In all, the group's nightfighter crews would make 33 claims in June and 27 in July, by which time RAF bombers had returned to more strategic targets in Germany.

The beginning of July had seen No 23 Sqn begin operations with No 100 Group alongside No 515 Sqn, both units specialising in performing low-level intruder missions which concentrated in the main on attacking enemy nightfighter bases.

On 20/21 July, No 169 Sqn's CO, Wg Cdr N B R Bromley, shot down a Bf 110 near Courtrai in FB VI NT113 (his third, and last, victory) to claim No 100 Group's 100th kill. The following month, on 8/9 August, squadronmate Flt Lt Tim Woodman, flying FB VI NT156/VI-Y, was supporting a raid on V1 sites in the Pas de Calais when he found an Fw 190, which was promptly chased. 'The Hun went downhill like the clappers', he later recalled, but Woodman shot it down nevertheless, claiming his fifth victory in the process. It was one of only eight kills achieved by the group's Mosquito force during the month, however.

Two of these victories fell to No 169 Sqn's 'Andy' Miller and Freddie Bone, who, on the 11th, scored their penultimate victory by destroying a Bf 109 near Dijon. The following night they claimed their 11th, and last, kill over Heligoland, as Miller explained to the Author;

'Freddie picked up a contact crossing slightly at quite a lick. We eventually caught up with it. Vertically above it, I identified it as an He 219. I dropped back to about 150 yards and gave it four two-second bursts. We were then hit by debris and lost coolant in both our engines. I glided in over the coast of Holland and Freddie baled out at 1200 ft and I followed at 800-900 ft.'

Both men were eventually captured, although Miller initially spent some time with the Dutch underground. When he was being interrogated, he met the pilot of the He 219 that he had shot down, enabling him to confirm his last victory! This was the first example of Heinkel's new nightfighter to fall to a Mosquito.

Having been hastily detached to West Malling to counter the V1 threat on 21 July, both Nos 85 and 157 Sqns returned to Swannington on 29 August. With six V1 kills to their credit following their spell flying ADGB missions, Sqn Ldr Ben Benson and Flt Lt Lewis Brandon scored No 157 Sqn's first nightfighter kills since June when they bagged a pair of Ju 88s on 11/12 September to take their own tally to seven destroyed.

Having scored three kills in Beaufighter VIs with No 125 Sqn in 1943, Flg Off 'Andy' Miller took his total to eleven during his time with No 169 Sqn flying the Mosquito on bomber support missions. The last of these victories, on 12 August 1944, took the form of the first He 219 nightfighter to be shot down by the RAF. Unfortunately, debris damage from the Heinkel caused the Mosquito crew to bale out, and they became PoWs (*David Ross*)

That same night No 85 Sqn's Sqn Ldr Branse Burbridge and Flt Lt Bill Skelton claimed a victory over the Baltic – probably Ju 88G-1 Wk-Nr 712195/ D9+BH of I./NJG 7.

Despite these renewed nightfighter successes, bomber-support Mosquito losses also continued to rise, and the following night Flg Offs W R Breithaupt and J A Kennedy of No 239 Sqn failed to return after clashing with a Bf 110. Post-war, the German crew who survived this action confirmed that they had also been shot down by their victim. Thus Bill Breithaupt became an ace posthumously.

Winter Nemesis

On 1 October 1944 the elite FIU had been re-established at part of the Night Fighter Development Wing (NFDW), the latter also including the Night Fighter Development Squadron (NFDS), the Fighter Interception Development Squadron (FIDS) and the Fighter Experimental Flight, which incorporated a *Ranger* flight. Amongst the personnel assigned to the NFDW were a dozen aces, spread amongst the various small elements that were controlled by the wing.

The formation of the NFDW served to further refine the greatly improved tactics that were being implemented by the nightfighter crews come the final winter of the war. The gradual wearing down of the enemy's air defence warning system led to increasing successes as 1944 drew to a close, and many of No 100 Group's leading aces increased their scores, as did some serving with Fighter Command's intruder units.

Among the latter was No 605 Sqn's Flg Off Roy Lelong, who became the unit's latest ace when, on the afternoon of 2 October, he conducted what was almost a personal vendetta against the Luftwaffe's seaplane force. In Great Jasmunder Bay, on the Baltic coast, he found no fewer than 13 Do 24s moored in the open, and as he recounted in his combat report;

'I went in very low, taking a Do 24 in the northern line first – flames could be seen licking up from part of the hull nearest the water. In all, seven attacks were carried out.'

In seven minutes of mayhem, he destroyed five Dorniers, damaged five and probably destroyed another on the water. Lelong and his navigator Plt Off J A McLaren then departed to the north, where they 'sighted a Bv 138 flying boat very low over the sea. I turned to starboard and closed to 150 yards, where the rear gunner opened fire and hit our port propeller. I then closed and fired a short burst which silenced the gunner. I followed through and sprayed the Bv with fire, and it was last seen in a turn with black smoke trailing from it'.

When the gun camera film was examined, Lelong was credited with having downed the Bv 138, making him an ace.

Late the following month No 605 Sqn moved to Hartfordbridge after being replaced at Manston by No 406 Sqn, which was led by future nine-kill ace Wg Cdr Russ Bannock. Although No 605 Sqn remained part of ADGB until war's end, the unit was re-designated an intruder squadron in late November and flew its first operation in this role on 5 December when five aircraft conducted an abortive mission to Holland.

At Swannington, No 85 Sqn received a considerable boost when Capt Svein Heglund arrived – he already had 12 and one shared day fighter

In late 1944 Capt Svein Heglund joined No 85 Sqn and claimed three Bf 110s destroyed in a month to take his victory tally to 15 and one shared destroyed. These successes made him the leading Norwegian fighter ace of World War 2 (*N Mathisrud*)

victories (on Spitfires with No 331 Sqn) to his credit, and he would end the war as the highest-scoring Norwegian ace. The first of his three night victories came on 4/5 December, as he wrote in his logbook;

'Escort for bombers bombing Karlsruhe and Heilbronn. Picked up several contacts around the airfield east of the target, but most seemed to be friendly. Bombing was very good. I got a contact on a Hun aircraft northeast of Heilbronn. I chased it for ten minutes. It was very dark, and I overshot it three times. I finally shot it down in flames far east of Heilbronn. We were shot at and hit by friendly flak over Brussels. They thought we were a "Doodle Bug". One Me 110 destroyed.'

Another of No 85 Sqn's future aces opened his score that same night when Flt Lt Dickie Goucher downed two Bf 110s, giving each several short bursts. Goucher's success was mirrored by his flight commander, Sqn Ldr 'Dolly' Doleman, who got his sixth and seventh kills. Finally, Flt Lt A J 'Ginger' Owen's 12th victory brought up No 85 Sqn's century!

Covering the same raid was No 157 Sqn's Flt Lt John Matthews, whose Ju 88 gave him his fourth kill. He achieved 'acedom' two nights later when he closed on a Bf 110 near Limberg after a 13-minute chase and opened fire from just 50 yards, scoring hits all over the fuselage. The Messerschmitt burst into flames and crashed. He quickly followed this up with a Ju 88 shortly afterwards.

On 6/7 December Flt Lt Edward Hedgecoe, who was attached to the NFDU *Ranger* Flight, closed on a Bf 110 and fired a two-second burst from 100 yards, causing the Messerschmitt to disintegrate and fall to earth. Six days later he shot down two more Bf 110s during a sortie over Germany to take his tally to nine destroyed. Hedgecoe was then promoted and sent to No 151 Sqn as a flight commander, only to be killed in a crash in bad weather on New Year's Day whilst flying his very first sortie with the unit.

Hedgecoe was the second Mosquito ace to be killed in the space of a fortnight, for 12 days earlier, on 18/19 December, eight-victory ace Flg Off Desmond Tull of the FIU had collided with a Bf 110 as the latter was coming in to land at Dusseldorf. The pilot of the German nightfighter, Hauptmann Breves, managed to land the badly damaged G9+CC of IV./NJG 1, but Tull and his navigator, Plt Off P J Cowgill, were killed.

Three days later on 22 December, the Swannington units had another

The Mosquito NF XIXs of No 157 Sqn – like MM652/RS-S, seen at Swannington after a heavy snowfall – achieved a considerable number of successes over Germany through the winter as the enemy's night defences weakened. MM652 subsequently served with No 169 Sqn, and it was eventually bought back by de Havilland in October 1948 and sold to the Swedish Air Force (*S Howe*)

Just west of Essen on the night of 12 December 1944, Sqn Ldr Branse Burbridge and Flt Lt Bill Skelton shot down this Bf 110G-4. It was probably G9+RT of 9./NJG 1, flown by Unteroffizier Rudolf Wilsch, who baled out with his crew. The Bf 110 was the 19th success for the No 85 Sqn crew (*B A Burbridge*)

successful night supporting bombing raids around Koblenz. Burbridge of No 85 Sqn and Doleman of No 157 Sqn each claimed a victory, the former shooting down Bf 110G-4 Wk-Nr 730349/2+PL of 3./NJG 6. However, the laurels that night went to 'Ginger' Owen, who made his final claims of the war when he shot down a Bf 110 and two Ju 88s to take his tally to 15 destroyed.

On Christmas Eve the No 100 Group Mosquitoes were again out in force, making their final claims of the year. At about 1830 hrs Sqn Ldr Ben Benson and Lewis Brandon shot down a Bf 110 near Mainz and Flt Lt John Matthews got a Ju 88G over Cologne. 'Dolly' Doleman and 'Bunny' Bunch were also in the thick of the action, engaging a Bf 110 over Cologne. Doleman recalled that 'The pride of the Luftwaffe caught fire immediately, but we gave him another burst just for fun'. Their victim was a significant 'scalp' – 56-victory *experte* and Knight's Cross holder Hauptmann Heinz Struning of 9./NJG 1, who was killed.

One of the most successful intruder teams was that of Sqn Ldr Russ Bannock (left) and Flg Off Robert Bruce (right) of No 418 Sqn. In addition to numerous aircraft destroyed in the air and on the ground, Bannock was credited with 18 and one shared V1s destroyed. He became an ace on Christmas Eve 1944 whilst serving as CO of No 406 Sqn. They are seen here posing in front of their FB VI HR147, nicknamed *HAIRLESS JOE*, at Middle Wallop in August 1944 (*Canadian Forces*)

The victorious crew then gained AI contact with 7./NJG 1's Bf 110 G9+GR, which they also shot down near Duisberg, and a later combat took their tally to three Bf 110s for the night. The new AI Mk X radar being used by both Nos 85 and 157 Sqns in its NF XIXs was clearly of benefit!

No 406 Sqn was also out intruding that night, receiving an early Christmas present when CO Russ Bannock, flying with 'Kirk' Kirkpatrick, flew to Paderborn. Bannock later recalled;

'We closed and easily identified a Ju 88, and in the bright moonlight we could even see its grey and blue camouflage. I opened fire just as it was turning on its approach. The port engine exploded and then the whole of the port wing caught fire and it did a gentle spiral to the left and crashed.'

This was the first of No 406 Sqn's intruding victories, and Bannock's sixth kill overall.

No 100 Group squadrons had claimed 38 enemy aircraft during December, and on the evening of 1 January 1945, whilst covering a raid against the Ruhr, Flt Lts Richard Goucher and 'Tiny' Bullock of No 85 Sqn shot down a Ju 88 after a lengthy chase. They then found a Ju 88G northeast of Dortmund, and firing a long burst from behind, 2Z+CP of 5./NJG 6 exploded, taking Goucher's total to five in less than a month. However, some debris hit the Mosquito when the second victim

No 515 Sqn's ebullient CO, Wg Cdr Howard Kelsey (left), shares a joke with his flight commander, Sqn Ldr Charles Winn. Kelsey made the final No 100 Group Mosquito claim on 24 April 1945 (*via Norman Franks*)

exploded and they had to limp back on one engine and make an emergency landing at Brussels.

The following night Branse Burbridge and Bill Skelton were flying, and they shot down a Ju 88 southwest of Ludwigshafen. This was Burbridge's 21st victory, making him the RAF's most successful nightfighter pilot. He recalled this mission for the Author;

'Flying west of Mannheim, Bill Skelton obtained a contact off to starboard at about our level – 15,000 ft. We closed in behind the aircraft, which was weaving gently and flying towards our target, Nuremburg. Bill identified it through our binoculars as a Ju 88, so I closed in and gave a short burst of no more than a half-second, which set the fuselage on fire. It then spiralled down in flames, breaking into three distinct burning pieces after it had exploded upon hitting the ground. On our return to base I found that we had fired just two-dozen rounds.'

On the night of 5/6 January the team of Ben Benson and Lewis Brandon had their final success when, during a high-level bomber support intruder mission to the Osnabruck area, they attacked an He 219 at 19,000 ft and sent it down northeast of Hannover.

Partly due to bad weather during January, all 13 of the No 100 Group victories for that month came in the first two weeks of the new year, and most of the ten claimed in February were also scored early on. One of the latter was claimed by No 515 Sqn's CO, Wg Cdr Howard Kelsey, who shot down a Ju 88 over Gutersloh for his seventh success on 2/3 February.

Despite an improvement in tactics by the No 100 Group Mosquito units, the enemy nightfighter arm still posed a serious threat, as both fighter and bomber losses proved. Indeed, on the night of 7 February Sqn Ldr Peter Bates of No 141 Sqn, who had five claims (including four confirmed), was shot down by a German nightfighter during a patrol to Landbergen.

With the increasingly critical shortage of fuel, which had a serious impact on the training of new crews, and the shrinking of the Reich itself, the Luftwaffe's nightfighter arm was coming under desperate pressure. The last 'throw of the dice' for the *Nachtjagd* came on the night of 3/4 March, when it went onto the offensive and despatched over 200 aircraft,

With its ASH radar fitted in the nose thimble, Mosquito FB VI RS566/3P-E belonged to No 515 Sqn, and was occasionally flown by the unit's very successful CO, Wg Cdr Howard Kelsey. His first mission in this aircraft was an uneventful patrol to Quackenbruck on 5 January 1945. Later serving with No 141 Sqn, RS566 was sold to the *Armée de l'Air* in August 1947 (*R W Elliott*)

including some 140 Ju 88s, on Operation *Gisela*. The German nightfighters succeeded in shooting down more than 20 returning RAF bombers over eastern England, and the three Ju 188s claimed by Nos 68 and 125 Sqns were a poor return. A significant number of enemy aircraft also crashed on their return flights, however.

Yet despite these losses, Bomber Command's night bomber offensive against Germany continued unabated, and two nights after *Gisela* No 239 Sqn's hugely experienced CO, Wg Cdr Walter Gibb, flew in support of a raid on Bohlen. Near Leipzig, he and his navigator Flt Lt R C Kendall picked up a contact on the AI, as Gibb recalled post-mission;

'A visual was identified as a Ju 88 flying cluelessly straight and level. I dropped back and fired a two-second burst, resulting in a large flash and debris flying off. I pulled up over the debris and was practically turned on my back by the slipstream. The Ju 88 dived away very steeply, well on fire, until visual was lost.'

Gibb had claimed another significant scalp, for he had shot down Oberstleutnant Walter Borchers of NJG 5 – a 59-victory *experte* and Knight's Cross holder. Four minutes later Flt Lt Kendall gained another contact. Gibb continued;

'It was chased towards Chemnitz and visual was obtained against cloud lit by the fires. We identified it as another Ju 88. Four bursts were fired in all, but this obstinate Hun refused to blow up. Debris came off and it went into a steep dive into cloud. Shortly afterwards the glow of an explosion was seen below.'

The pair continued on patrol before heading for home, Walter Gibb having become the RAF's latest ace.

The intruders from both Fighter Command and No 100 Group also continued to be active, although these missions continued to prove hazardous, as was again shown on 17 March when No 605 Sqn's CO, Wg Cdr R A 'Mitch' Mitchell, went missing whilst attacking enemy transport routes in Germany. A very successful pilot, Mitchell had five and three shared victories to his name.

It is perhaps appropriate that the last nightfighter pilot to become an ace belonged to one of the longest serving and most successful nightfighting units of them all. No 85 Sqn's Flt Lt H B Thomas had scored his first victory in October 1943, and he finally claimed his fifth victim on 8 April 1945 when he downed a Ju 88 west of Lutzkendorf. He later recalled;

'I saw a bomber going down in flames and I decided that there was a fair chance of there being at least one Hun in the area – and this proved to be the case, for within a few seconds we had an AI contact slightly below us. We turned in behind it and followed the contact. From a distance of about 800 ft I could identify it clearly as a Ju 88. I fired one burst from dead astern with no deflection and this produced a very bright explosion, causing it to shed pieces and lose speed very quickly. I orbited to port and

This NF XXX (NT242/RS-F) of No 157 Sqn was named *Fairynuff* and decorated with this very attractive artwork during its brief service with the squadron. Having previously served with Nos 239 and 85 Sqns, NT242 finished its RAF service with No 502 Sqn post-war. It was redesignated a maintenance airframe in May 1949 (*M Goodman*)

awaited the prang – this occurred in a very satisfactory manner when it hit the ground with a beautiful explosion over the Thuringian Plain.'

Hugh Thomas was shot down by an enemy nightfighter five days later after one engine of his Mosquito had been knocked out in error by a Lancaster gunner. Baling out, he became a PoW, but sadly his navigator, Flg Off C B Hamilton, landed in the sea and was lost.

In spite of the Third Reich disintegrating, there was still some 'trade' for the bomber support and intruders. On 14 April No 239 Sqn claimed its 55th, and final, victory, as described in its operations book. 'Sqn Ldr Dennis Raby (in NF XXX NT330) shot down a Ju 88 that had been neatly coned by its own searchlights over Berlin for him!' It was his fourth victory. Ten days later Russ Bannock claimed No 406 Sqn's last when he downed a Ju 88 over Wittstock. The following night, 24/25 April, No 515 Sqn's CO, Wg Cdr Howard Kelsey, got a Do 217 over Libeznice, near Prague. He thus gained the unique distinction of claiming both the first and the last kills for No 100 Group's nightfighters, the first being in a Beaufighter.

Things then began to run down, with No 85 Sqn flying its final operations of the war on the night of 2 May when three Mosquitoes performed a bomber support mission and one made a low level intruder to Grosenbrode. Nos 157 and 239 Sqns also flew their last that night, as did No 515 Sqn when Kelsey led an attack on Sylt airfield. That same night No 406 Sqn's Flt Lt John Caine, who was the leading RCAF intruder pilot, hit Marrebeck airfield in Denmark, where he strafed and destroyed two Ju 52/3ms and his wingman got four more. These were the RCAF's last intruder claims. The various Mosquito squadrons truly had been the *Nachtjagd's* Nemesis.

CHAPTER FIVE

OVER MOUNTAINS AND JUNGLE

The first Mosquito to reach the Mediterranean was PR I W4055, flown by Sqn Ldr Rupert Clerke, which landed in Malta following a reconnaissance of Italy on 4 November 1941. It would be just over a year before Mosquitoes appeared on the embattled islands for more active operations.

During the afternoon of 6 December 1942, No 23 Sqn was unexpectedly withdrawn from intruder operations. The following day it began to take delivery of new Mosquito NF IIs fitted with overload tanks. With the hasty completion of fuel consumption tests, the aircraft began flying out to Malta on 21 December, as the squadron CO, Wg Cdr Peter Wykeham-Barnes, later recalled;

'Jack Starr and I were awakened at 0100 hrs, and we looked out onto a brilliant moon and clear sky. At 0400 hrs DZ230 "A-Apple" taxied out to the take-off point, followed by the rest of the squadron, and we rose into the starlit sky and then headed out towards the Scilly Isles, lying black in the path of the moon. Two hours later the sun rose on the left out of the mountains of Spain, showing the Bay of Biscay lying calm and milky 15,000 ft below. As the early rays glinted off the airscrews, and after a short cut, Gibraltar was sighted four hours and ten minutes after take-off. One by one the squadron came in on the tricky racecourse runway, and the crews assembled for a late breakfast.

'On 27 December orders were received to move to Malta, six aircraft at a time, and to go at once. The first party made one circuit of the Rock, and without waiting even to form up, set course for Algiers, refuelled and left at dusk for Malta. One circuit and "A-Apple" touched down on Luqa runway, the first Mosquito fighter in Malta.'

Soon afterwards Wykeham-Barnes flew the squadron's first intruder to eastern Sicily, although no activity was seen due to bad weather.

The squadron was an important addition to Malta's air arsenal, which was in the process of switching to more offensive operations. No 23 Sqn's first success from there came on 7 January 1943, as described by Wykeham-Barnes;

'The score was opened by Jack Starr, who, at Castel Vetrano, caught up with a Ju 52/3m coming in to land and gave it a squirt. The Hun took evasive action by blowing up into a thousand pieces, and "E-Evelyn" (DD687/YP-E) flew through the bits, with the crew temporarily blinded by the explosion. This caused "A" Flight to wear a slightly superior look, but "Rusty" (Sqn Ldr S P Russell) evened the score two nights later when he found a Ju 88 and set in on fire after a short running fight. He watched it crash into the sea.'

The squadron also now ranged over southern Italy too, taking a toll of ground targets. On 1 February two Mosquitoes (one flown by future ace

Sqn Ldr 'Jackie' Starr of No 23 Sqn became an accomplished intruder pilot, destroying five aircraft in the air. Sadly, he was killed in a flying accident in January 1945 (*Peter Rudd*)

Plt Off Leo Williams, patrolled Pantelleria and Comiso. Williams achieved his first success during the mission when he destroyed a Ju 88 as it landed at Comiso, while his CO forced Pantelleria to close down for one-and-a-half hours. The following night 'Jackie' Starr flew No 23 Sqn's first intruder to Naples. By month-end five enemy aircraft had been shot down by the unit, which had also caused considerable disruption to the enemy.

Another significant character joined No 23 Sqn at this time too in the shape of Flg Off Arthur Hodgkinson, who already had nine Blenheim and Beaufighter victories to his credit from a previous tour with No 219 Sqn. He was soon scoring again, as the unit's operational log for 15 March records;

'Heavy rains flooded the dispersal and went a long way to dampening the ardour of the squadron, but Flg Off Hodgkinson cheered everybody up by destroying an He 111 at Catania. He saw several aircraft during the patrol and made another attack, but saw no result.'

Five weeks later, on 26/27 April, he was credited with two Ju 88s destroyed that were the 998th and 999th victims for the Malta fighter defences. Sadly, the prize for the 1000th eluded No 23 Sqn!

As the campaign in North Africa reached its climax, the squadron's Mosquito intruders maintained the pressure on the enemy's air bases in Sicily, keeping them closed and increasing the losses and general stress on

When No 23 Sqn moved to Malta in December 1942, Mosquito NF II DZ230/YP-A was flown by the CO, Wg Cdr Peter Wykeham-Barnes. He also flew the unit's first sortie over Sicily in it. His regular aircraft, Wykeham-Barnes shot down two Ju 88s flying DZ230, taking his final score to 14 and 3 shared destroyed. This aircraft was written off when it overshot the runway on landing at Luqa on 22 June 1943 (*Peter Rudd*)

Another of No 23 Sqn's early Mosquito NF IIs was DZ228/YP-D, which was ferried out by Flt Lt Tym and usually flown by one of the unit's Polish crews, consisting of Flt Lt Orzenowski and Flg Off Szponarowicz. It was posted missing on a sortie from Luqa on 21 January 1943 (*via John Hamlin*)

Wg Cdr Peter Wykeham-Barnes (right), who led No 23 Sqn with distinction from Malta, is seen here in a casual pose with the AOC Malta, Air Vice Marshal Sir Keith Park, who was himself a 20-victory ace from World War 1 (*Peter Rudd*)

enemy crews. No 23 Sqn's casualties were not light during this period, however, as Wykeham-Barnes noted;

'Johnny Streibel three times brought his machine home on one engine. Jack Starr's "E-Evelyn", savaged by flak and hit in the radiator and wings, came home successfully and flew again in a very short time, while another machine had a 20 mm shell clean through the fuselage, apparently with little effect.'

The pressure was maintained in May when 233 sorties were flown, 175 of them intruder patrols during which six enemy aircraft were destroyed, as well as a large number of locomotives and other targets, although at a cost of seven aircraft. The squadron also began receiving fighter-bomber FB VIs at this time, and after Wykeham-Barnes had suffered a ruptured knee cartilage doing physical exercise(!), the unit received a new CO when Wg Cdr John Selby, who had four victories from the desert fighting, took over. He flew his first patrol on 8 May – an intruder to eastern Sicily.

Events in the Mediterranean now crowded in. Axis forces in North Africa surrendered on 13 May, and a month later the garrisons on the small, but important, Italian islands of Pantelleria, Lampedusa and Linosa also fell, and the plans for the invasion of Sicily proceeded.

NIGHT KILLS

In order to provide additional night protection for the planned invasion of Sicily, on 1 July Ford-based No 256 Sqn was ordered to send a detachment of six Mosquito NF XIIs to Luqa, and fitted with long-range tanks, they left the following evening. The pilots involved were Sqn Ldr J W Allan, Plt Off L G Searle, Flt Sgt Beachcraft, Flg Off S R Robinson, Sgt Costley and Sgt Jenkins. Five NF XIIs eventually arrived at Luqa, with the sixth crash-landing at Krendi. They were the first radar-equipped Mosquito nightfighters to be sent to Malta. The detachment was parented by No 108 Sqn, which was then flying Beaufighters.

D-Day for the landings on Sicily – code named Operation *Husky* – was on 10 July, and the date saw a 'maximum effort' put up by both No 23 Sqn and the No 256 Sqn detachment. The former flew intruders over southern Italy, while the nightfighters conducted protection patrols. Late the following evening, Flg Off Jack Robinson and Flt Sgt K H Midgely of No 256 Sqn, in NF II HK133, were on patrol when they were vectored towards some bandits. The squadron diary recorded, 'Identified a Ju 88. Opened fire at 700-800 ft, enemy aircraft dived away to starboard, the dive becoming steeper until it hit the ground and blew up. Returned to patrol, then base'. It was the start of an astonishing run of success for the detachment.

Robinson was successful again the following night, although his efforts were somewhat overshadowed by Sqn Ldr J W 'Ian' Allan, who, with his Australian navigator Flg Off H J Davidson, in NF II HK131 destroyed a Ju 88 and a Cant Z1007bis – this was the first of 14 victories for the pair in an incredible few weeks. The detachment diary noted;

'Patrolled area of Syracuse under control of "Blackbeer". After vectors, obtained contact at two miles – closed to visual range after a hectic chase and identified it as a Ju 88. Fired one-second burst from dead astern at 150 ft range and enemy aircraft exploded and dived into the sea off Cape Marro di Porco, where it burned for some time. Confirmed on R/T by

"Sweetheart" (aboard the naval vessel HMS *Butolo*). After further patrolling, we received information that the bogey was travelling south towards Mosquito. We gained contact at three miles and obtained visual of a Cant Z1007. I fired a one second burst from 50 ft and the port engine caught fire and return fire was experienced. The enemy aircraft dived violently, and another burst from 1000 ft set it well alight and a third burst from 200 ft caused it to explode and dive into the sea, lighting up the sky when striking the water. Both these victories were confirmed by Wg Cdr Green of No 600 Sqn.'

On 13/14 July Plt Off Searle got an He 111 and a Ju 88, one of which also fell to Allan over Sicily, who, with Davidson, was airborne again shortly after 0100 hrs on the 16th. Ordered to patrol area 'Bark', by the time they landed at 0500 hrs they had joined a rather exclusive club, as the operation log again sets out;

'0300 hrs – Contact at three-and-a-half miles well above, "bogey" taking mild evasive action – closed to 100 ft dead astern and identified as a Cant Z1007bis. Gave a one second burst from 100 ft dead astern and the tail fell off. The aircraft spun down blazing, hit the sea and exploded. Confirmed by "Sweetheart" on R/T.

'0335 hrs – Contact at about three-and-a-half miles on an evading target. Closed to visual range and identified a Ju 88 – enemy aircraft must have seen me, turned to port and commenced to dive. Gave him a one second burst at 30 degrees angle off. Cockpit of the enemy aircraft exploded and it dived vertically. Tried to follow him down but held contact down to 1000 ft. Did not see him actually hit the sea, but saw blazing wreckage on the sea two seconds later.'

The destruction of the Ju 88 had elevated 'Ian' Allan to ace status in just four days! Yet more was to follow, as the log continues;

'0414 hrs – Northeast of Augusta. Contact at about two-and-a-half miles range on evading target well below. Closed to 500 ft below and behind and identified a Ju 88. Gave a half-second burst from close dead astern, setting the starboard engine and fuselage alight, then gave a second

Prior to the invasion of Sicily, No 256 Sqn sent out a small detachment of Mosquito NF XII nightfighters to Malta, of which HK128/JT-G was one, and they made a huge contribution to the success of the operation. This particular aircraft was often flown by Flg Off Jack Robinson, who had made the detachment's first claim. The fighter is also thought to have been flown by the unit's most successful pilot, Sqn Ldr J W Allan, who on 16 July became an 'ace in a night'. HK128 had previously served with No 219 Sqn prior to being issued to No 256 Sqn, and it was still flying with the latter unit when it was written off in an accident on 21 May 1944 (*B J Wild*)

burst, whereupon another explosion on the port motor and the whole aircraft flamed brightly, turned on its back and dived toward the sea. Two parachutes were seen at this point. The aircraft hit the sea with a brilliant flash.

'0440 hrs – Northeast of Syracuse. Contact well below at 5000 ft head on, crossed scan and off turn orbited hard to port. Regained contact at 9000 ft range, dropped to 7000 ft height behind him and closed, the enemy aircraft taking standard evasive action of 30 degrees weave either side. Identified as a Ju 88. One short burst from 100 ft dead astern, when he blew up and broke into pieces that hit the sea blazing.'

Allen then destroyed a fourth Ju 88 to give him 'ace in a night' status. This feat also saw him become the first pilot to achieve five in a single sortie on the Mosquito. The following night the pair shot down another two Cant Z1007s over Sicily, and after this astonishing run of ten victories in four days Allan was awarded a well deserved immediate DSO – DFCs for both he and his navigator would follow in August.

No 23 Sqn continued to be active too, as during the moon period they flew some very effective intruders. On the 20th Paul Rabone attacked a seaplane base on Lake Bracciano, near Rome, and damaged three Ca 506 floatplanes in the longest intruder mission undertaken by the squadron to that time. That same night Wg Cdr John Selby destroyed an He 111 near Lecce for his fifth, and final, victory.

However it was a night of mixed fortunes, as 12-kill ace Arthur Hodgkinson was lost near Rome, as the diarist wrote. '"Hodge" was on his 49th intruder sortie, and had achieved a record of outstanding quality'. The following day another aircraft, flown by Flt Lt Innes and Plt Off Lord, was lost in the Rome area.

In spite of what it seemed, not every aircraft that 'Ian' Allan encountered fell – on the 19th he had intercepted one that manoeuvred violently and then out-climbed the Mosquito to escape. It might possibly have been an Me 410. Nonetheless, by the end of the month three more bombers had fallen to his fire, while other No 256 Sqn pilots had also made claims.

The pace of success reduced somewhat during August, when several of the notable pilots of both units claimed. On the 15th it was noted of the newly promoted Sqn Ldr Rabone that;

In July 1943 Mosquito FB VI HJ675/YP-V became the regular aircraft of Flt Lt Paul Rabone, who flew his first intruder in it on the 6th of that month. Exactly two weeks later he damaged three seaplanes near Rome on No 23 Sqn's longest intruder to that date. Rabone finally became an ace whilst flying HJ675 on 8 September when he brought down a Ju 88 near Grosseto. He also shot down an He 111 and damaged a second Heinkel bomber during the same mission (*Peter Rudd*)

New Zealander Flt Lt Paul Rabone (left) was a hugely experienced nightfighter pilot, having made his first night claim flying Hurricanes during the Blitz. He later flew Defiants, Havocs and Beaufighters, but most of his successes came after converting to Mosquito intruders. He was lost in action serving with No 23 Sqn in the UK when, on 24 July 1944, he failed to return from an intruder mission over Germany (*Peter Rudd*)

In October 1944 No 256 Sqn came under the control of 23-year-old Wg Cdr H W 'Chubby' Eliot, who had six and one shared victories to his credit. He added two more kills (his final claims) in intruder sorties over Greece soon after becoming CO. Eliot led from the front, and was shot down by flak and killed when attacking a bridge on the night of 4 March 1945 (*via C F Shores*)

'He borrowed a Spitfire to convey spare parts for the Mosquito detachment at Palermo. On his return he encountered and shot down a Ju 88, which was on a recce off Trapani. This breach of good manners adds a new aircraft to the usual operational types flown by the squadron!'

On the 30th Sqn Ldr Allan made his 14th, and final, claim when he shot down his fifth Cant Z1007bis in flames.

LACK OF TARGETS

Following the fall of Sicily, the Allies had quickly crossed the Messina Straits into Italy, and on 8 September 1943 they carried out another landing at Salerno, to the south of Naples, which was to result in the Italian capitulation. In support of Operation *Avalanche*, No 23 Sqn, by now mainly flying FB VIs, fielded nine crews to close all enemy airfields in the Foggia and Rome areas that night.

Hours earlier, over Grossetto, Rabone, who had made his first claim during the Battle of Britain in a No 145 Sqn Hurricane, was finally elevated to 'acedom' when he shot down a Ju 88 and an He 111.

To further enhance the nightfighter defences in the Mediterranean, at the end of the month the rest of No 256 Sqn began moving to Malta to join the highly successful detachment. However, there was now a marked decrease in enemy air activity, and in late October No 23 Sqn moved forward to Pomigliano, near Naples. It began operations on 1 November when the recently arrived CO, Wg Cdr Burton-Gyles, flew an intruder to the Viterbo area. That month No 256 Sqn began receiving Mosquito NF XIIIs, and it remained committed to the day and night defence of Malta until April 1944, holding crews at readiness round the clock for this and convoy protection work.

For No 23 Sqn, its main focus shifted to intruder attacks on enemy logistics and communications, while the crews of No 256 Sqn were left to fly relatively uneventful nocturnal patrols. However, a major action came on 21 December 1943 when six Ju 88s attacked a convoy and were intercepted by two Mosquitoes, which managed to destroy one of them.

At the end of January 1944, No 23 Sqn recorded that it had destroyed 33 enemy aircraft in the air and 39 on the ground, as well as a large number of other ground targets, since arriving in Malta. No 256 Sqn, although it remained at Luqa, also flew from Catania, in Sicily, on convoy escorts patrols, but in February it also joined No 23 Sqn in flying intruders. That month, too, to their great delight, 'B' Flight of No 108 Sqn received three Mosquitoes, only to be told that it would remain equipped with Beaufighters! Its first Mosquito operation was on 5 April, but they were withdrawn in July.

In early April No 256 Sqn moved to La Senia, in Algeria, from where it shot down two Ju 88s during May, while No 23 Sqn began Day *Ranger* flights over France at this time. The first two were flown by Sqn Ldr Russell and Flg Off Badley, who destroyed a Do 217 and damaged two others at Perpignan. On 1 May Russell damaged a Ju 188, which proved to be the unit's last claim in the theatre, as a few days later No 23 Sqn was withdrawn to the UK for night bomber support duties as part of No 100 Group.

On 15 August 1944 No 256 Sqn moved to Alghero, on the island of Sardinia, but it transferred again in late September to Foggia, on the

Italian east coast, from where it began operations over the Balkans on day and night *Rangers*. On 1 October Wg Cdr Hugh 'Chubby' Eliot assumed command. He was already an ace with six and one shared victories to his name, having seen action in France and Malta in 1940-41, followed by command of No 255 Sqn in 1943-44. The new CO flew his first trip on the 4th, with navigator Flt Lt Denis Ibbotson, on an intruder to Salonika, and as the squadron records relate, he met with immediate success;

'We observed a Ju 52 with its landing light burning in the circuit, making its final approach at approximately 400 ft. I gave two short bursts at 500 yards, closing to 150 yards with deflection on a beam attack. The enemy aircraft burst into flames, crashing just off the end of the runway. We resumed the patrol, and it was still burning vigorously when we came off patrol at 2225 hrs.'

'Chubby' Eliot had begun his tour in style! His was not, however, the only success, as one of his flight commanders, Sqn Ldr Mumford, got a Ju 88, while Flt Sgt McEwan bagged an He 111 with only seven rounds per gun – both these pilots were breaking their duck.

Two nights later Eliot and Ibbotson were one of three intruder crews sent to Athens, via Brindisi, where they refuelled. Eliot landed back at 0200 hrs and reported;

'On patrol Athens area at 2310 hrs, we sighted an aircraft with nav lights on at 500 ft and closed in from 500 yards and gave a full deflection short burst without seeing any result. The aircraft was observed to be a large three-engined flying boat. We orbited to deliver a second attack, with the enemy aircraft now on an easterly course at 500 ft without nav lights(!), but very bright exhausts were seen, so enabling our Mosquito to intercept and deliver a second attack at 500 yards at full deflection, but with no visible results.

'We then made further attacks, following the enemy aircraft on a southeast course approximately one mile inside the coastline and identified the contact as a Do 24. We delivered a long burst from dead astern at a rapidly closing range. Many strikes were observed on and around the port engine. The enemy aircraft burst into flames, so we banked away and orbited. The enemy aircraft attempted to ditch but crashed onto the water's edge and exploded.'

The flying boat was from KTB *HeeresGruppe* E, and it was 'Chubby' Eliot's ninth, and last, victory.

The winter rain and mud caused considerable interference to operations, but No 256 Sqn nevertheless managed to open its 'book' for 1945 on 3 January when a Ju 188 fell to its guns. Other squadrons in the area were also re-equipping with Mosquito nightfighters. At Cesnatico, north of Rimini, No 600 Sqn (the RAF's most successful nightfighter squadron) was one such unit. Its new CO, Wg Cdr A H Drummond, flew the squadron's first patrol in a NF XIX on 22 January 1945, and had their first, inconclusive, encounter with the enemy near Venice on 16 February.

On 4 March No 256 Sqn suffered a great loss when, during a night intruder, its 23-year-old CO, 'Chubby' Eliot, with Flt Lt Cox, was shot down and killed by flak while attacking a bridge.

Bomber support, intruders and nightfighter patrols occupied all the squadrons through March. In support of the Bostons of No 232 Wing,

By early 1945 several additional Italy-based units had begun to receive Mosquito nightfighters, including No 255 Sqn at Foggia. The unit's first NF XIX (TA428/YD-A) is seen here undergoing its acceptance checks during January. This aircraft served exclusively with the unit, and was struck off charge the following year (*No 255 Sqn Records*)

newly-transitioned No 255 Sqn began patrols off the Po, and on the 21st Flg Off John Scollen shot down a Ju 88 off Trieste – his third, and final, victory with the squadron. The following night Flt Lt Pertwee and Flt Sgt F E Smith downed a Ju 188, these victories being No 255 Sqn's last, taking its final total to 95 destroyed.

The enemy only ventured over the lines on three nights during April, such was the paucity of his assets. No 255 Sqn countered with some of its new NF XXXs, the first patrol taking place on the night of the 11th. Twenty-four hours later, Sqn Ldr G W Hammond of 600 Sqn shot down an Fw 190 near Alfonsine, as he outlined at the time;

'Patrolled near Ravenna and was told of a bogey at 9000 ft. We gained AI contact and visual on two aircraft approaching from "ten o'clock", passing overhead 2000 ft above. I turned hard about and climbed, closing to 300 yards, and identified two Fw 190s. The leader was flying straight and climbing, the No 2 weaving gently out to starboard. I closed to 300 yards and opened fire on the leader, seeing a good concentration of strikes and a centrally underslung long range belly tank burst into flames. There was a large explosion as the Fw 190 turned slowly to starboard and went straight down. When last seen, it was disappearing into ten-tenths cloud at 7000 ft and still burning furiously. Claim one Fw 190 destroyed.'

This was No 600 Sqn's final victory of the war, and it was also the last for the Mosquito in the Mediterranean.

OVER THE JUNGLE

The first Mosquitoes to arrive in India were a few delivered for trials with Beaufighter VIF-equipped No 27 Sqn in mid 1943, although the unit was never fully equipped. However, in February 1944 No 45 Sqn at Yelahanka began swapping its Vengeance I/IIs for Mosquito FB VIs, and No 82 Sqn made a similar swap at Kolar in July.

The Mosquitoes were to fly in support of the advance through Burma on long-range fighter-bomber sorties, striking deep at Japanese lines of communication. With the enemy offering only a minimal aerial presence, the opportunities for air combat were therefore few.

Part of the newly re-titled No 908 Wing, No 45 Sqn flew its first offensive Mosquito missions on 1 October when Flt Lt C S Emeny led a sweep over several Japanese airfields that appeared to be unused, although a Ki-48 'Lily' bomber was shared damaged at Nawngkio. The unit quickly got into its stride, launching about eight sorties a day, and on the 6th, at Heho, it found a Ki-46 'Dinah' that was blown up and destroyed. However, the Mosquitoes were grounded shortly afterwards following several structural failures.

The squadron resumed operations on 9 November, when seven Mosquitoes mounted a dawn raid on Meiktila. Bad weather meant that only four got there, and they encountered Japanese fighters for the first time in the shape of Ki-43 'Oscars' and Ki-44 'Tojos'. Flg Off Pete Ewing was hit by flak and then attacked by an 'Oscar', but he managed to easily outrun the latter. However, Flt Lt Emeny and Canadian Wt Off Yanota were attacked and shot down by a Ki-43 and became PoWs. In an attempt to even up the score, Plt Off Nick Nichols then attacked the 'Oscar' and claimed hits on its wings.

No 82 Sqn began operations in mid December, while on Boxing Day No 45 Sqn destroyed a Ki-46 'Dinah' at Heho. Three days later, during an attack on Meiktila, No 45 Sqn again encountered enemy fighters when six 'Oscars' and a solitary 'Tojo' intercepted them. One Ki-43 got onto the tail of a Mosquito, but fortunately Wt Off Walsh, flying FB VI HR456/OB-M, intervened, although whether the fighter was shot down or damaged is unclear. The squadron again clashed with Ki-43s over Meiktila on 15 January, when Flt Lt Goodwin's aircraft was shot down.

On 4 February No 45 Sqn sent out eight 'Rhubarbs'. As dawn was breaking over Heho, Flg Off Pete Ewing and Wt Off 'Pinkie' Pinkerton spotted a Ki-21 'Sally' taking off. The squadron recorded the detail of what proved to be the last Mosquito victory in Burma;

'Switching to guns, the aircraft was attacked at 500 ft, fire being opened at 1000 yards, closing to 200 yards, and the enemy aircraft burst into flames and was totally destroyed.'

With the expansion of the Mosquito force in Burma, a number of veteran fighter pilots from Europe were also posted in to serve with the various units. In February 1945, No 74 Sqn Battle of Britain Spitfire ace Flt Lt Bryan Draper was posted to No 45 Sqn, but sadly on the 28th, when attacking a Japanese camp, his Mosquito was seen to break up at 4000 ft in its dive, crash and burn.

The Mosquito saw very little aerial combat on the Burma front, with the type's last claim being made by Flg Off Pete Ewing RAAF (left) and his navigator, Flt Sgt 'Pinkie' Pinkerton (right), on 3 February 1945, when they shot down a Ki-21 'Sally' just after it had taken off from Heho airfield. Three months earlier, this pair had also had an encounter with some Ki-43 'Oscars', but they had used the Mosquito's speed to escape the Japanese fighters (*A N Huon*)

The first Mosquito nightfighters in the Far East went to No 89 Sqn, to which NF XIX TA192/Q belonged. Sqn Ldr Allan Browne, who had found success flying with No 488 Sqn in the UK, arrived to help conversion, and in the immediate aftermath of the Japanese surrender he became the CO (*via J J Halley*)

Two months later six-kill Beaufighter and Mosquito ace Flt Lt John Etherton, who had previously flown with Nos 89 and 151 Sqns, was posted to the recently equipped No 176 Sqn, with whom he flew cover to the sea-borne landings at Rangoon on 1 May.

Later that month the first Mosquito NF XIX nightfighters began arriving with No 89 Sqn at Baigachi. Sqn Ldr Allen Browne, who had four Mosquito victories from his tour with No 488 Sqn, was posted in to assist with the conversion, and he later commanded the unit. In mid June ace Wg Cdr Michael Constable-Maxwell arrived, with Flt Lt John Quinton as his navigator, to take command of No 84 Sqn. Three months later he led the squadron's section of the Victory flypast over Kuala Lumpur. That month No 47 Sqn also gained a new CO with a successful air combat record when Wg Cdr George Melville-Jackson arrived.

Both of these squadrons sent detachments to Java for action against separatist rebels during November, Constable-Maxwell and Quinton bombing targets in Sourabaya on the 12th. Later in the day they bombed the Hotel Brunet, Sourabaya, in poor weather and strafed a machine gun pit, following which bodies were seen. A Bofors-gun position was also strafed and hits made on houses in the nearby area. They noted that the tracer fire from the positions was accurate!

No 47 Sqn also saw action in Java, Melville-Jackson noting in his log book entry for the 28th, 'Army Escort. Raid on Bekassi village. Hit by 0.303-in starboard inner petrol tank'. The following day he flew cover for troops east of Batavia. A roadblock was seen and they demolished a strongpoint. On the 30th Melville-Jackson flew a strike on a position east of Anbarawa, with the four aircraft firing 60-lb rocket projectiles. He recorded in his log book, 'Led eight Mossies and four T/bolts on raid on gun positions Ambarawa. Whole area strafed. Confirmed successful by Army'. The RAF's Mosquito detachment continued on these duties until early 1946, when they were withdrawn.

Coastal fighter ace Wg Cdr George Melville-Jackson became the CO of No 47 Sqn in 1945, and duly led the unit on operations in Java against Indonesian separatists post-war (*G H Melville-Jackson*)

Mosquito FB VI RF942/KU-H of No 47 Sqn is loaded with rocket projectiles during the Java operation. It was flown on several strikes during this period by Wg Cdr Melville-Jackson (*via G J Thomas*)

EPILOGUE

By the spring of 1945, the night skies of Germany belonged to the Mosquito nightfighters and intruders of Fighter Command, the 2nd TAF and No 100 Group, who almost roamed at will. The night of 24/25 April saw No 515 Sqn's CO, Howard Kelsey, catch a Do 217 at Libeznice, near Prague, just after it took off for his ninth kill – this was also the last victory for No 100 Group. That same night, the unit that claimed the first Mosquito victory, No 151 Sqn, also wrapped up its 'bag', while another long serving unit, No 264 Sqn, made its final claim when Plt Off Hutton shot down an Fw 190 over Berlin.

Twenty-four hours later, shortly before dawn, Mosquito NF XXX NT527 of No 488 Sqn, flown by Flg Offs John Marshall and Philip Prescott, set up a patrol in the Wittenburg area in clear moonlight under control of a mobile GCI. Marshall recorded the subsequent events in his combat report;

'After we came under GCI control at 0425 hrs, we patrolled for five minutes when the controller told us of a "bogey" crossing port to starboard six miles ahead and flying very slowly. The controller vectored us round until we were behind the target at a height of 1000 ft. My navigator then picked up contact at two miles range, "eleven o'clock", our height then being 1000 ft. I closed very rapidly, using 30 degrees of flap and making a speed of only 150 mph. I obtained a visual on target at 2000 ft range, "twelve o'clock" and 30 degrees above. The target was then taking evasive action consisting of 30 degree weaves on a mean course of 270. My navigator, using night binoculars, confirmed my identification that the target was an Fw 189, from 700 ft range.

'Just at that time the target apparently became aware of our presence and commenced to take violent evasive action. I followed the target, and just as it commenced what looked to be a peel off to starboard, I fired a two- to three-second burst at 200 yards range and 30 degrees deflection. Strikes were observed on the cockpit and the port boom, and large flashes

No 151 Sqn claimed the Mosquito's first confirmed victories in 1942. On 6 May 1945, in the hands of Flt Lt D W Shaw, NF XXX NT306/DZ-D, seen here in unfortunate circumstances, flew the squadron's final wartime sortie – a freelance patrol. This photograph was taken on 11 September 1946, after the fighter had overshot the runway at Odiham when its pilot attempted an engine-out landing – note the angle of the propeller blades for the inoperable right engine. The fighter hit a hedge and broke its back (*RAFM*)

Mosquito NF XXX NT484/VY-B was delivered to No 85 Sqn on 8 March 1945, and during that month it was flown on several operations by the most successful Norwegian fighter pilot of World War 2, Capt Svein Heglund. It also participated in No 85 Sqn's final wartime operation in May (*P H T Green collection*)

were seen in the cockpit. The enemy aircraft did not catch fire but straightened up first, then turned on its back at 1800 ft and dived vertically into the ground, where it exploded and continued to burn.'

The crew returned to base at 0650 hrs, where they proudly posted their second victory. It was No 488 Sqn's last of the war, for the squadron disbanded the following day and, perhaps more significantly, this Fw 189 – a type rarely encountered by the western Allies – was also the last victory in the air claimed by the elegant and deadly Mosquito in World War 2.

It was not the last damage that the de Havilland twin inflicted on the Luftwaffe, however, as the intruders continued to destroy what was left of the once mighty German air force on the ground. In the early hours of 3 May Flg Off John Caine, the leading RCAF intruder pilot of the war, hit Marrebeck airfield, in Denmark, where he destroyed two Ju 52/3ms and his wingman got four more – the last RCAF intruder kills.

The previous day one of the RAF's longest serving and most successful nightfighter units, No 85 Sqn, flew its final operations when three Mosquitoes performed a bomber support operation and one made a low level intruder to Grosenbrode. It numbered amongst its alumni some of the most successful Mosquito nightfighter pilots of the war, including no less than 20 aces. It is perhaps appropriate, therefore, that the last word should go to one of them – the most successful Mosquito pilot of them all, and the leading Allied nightfighter pilot of the war, Wg Cdr Branse Burbridge, who told the Author;

'The Mosquito was a quite superb aircraft, but could be tricky to fly, especially on one engine. In a word, successful nightfighting was down to one thing – teamwork.

'We owed a huge amount to our groundcrews, something that is often overlooked. However, any success that I achieved was due in large part to my navigator and life-long friend, Bill Skelton. He was magnificent.'

The most successful RAF (and Allied!) nightfighter pilot, with 21 confirmed victories, was Wg Cdr Branse Burbridge (right), who attributed much of this success to his navigator, and lifelong friend, Sqn Ldr Bill Skelton (left). Both were decorated with the DSO and bar and the DFC and bar (*B A Burbridge*)

APPENDICES

MOSQUITO ACES

Name	Service	Sqn/s	Mosquito Claims	Total	Theatre/s
B A Burbridge	RAF	85/NFLS	21/1/1 +3 V1s	21/2/1 +3 V1s	UK
W P Green	RAF	85/410/96/219	14/-/- +13 V1s	14/-/- +13 V1s	UK
J W Allan	RAF	256/151/29	14/-/-	14/-/-	UK/ME
C C Scherf	RAAF	418	13.5/-/-	13.5/-/-	UK
R D Doleman	RAF	157/125/264	10+2sh/1/0.5 +3 V1s	10+2sh/1/0.5 +3 V1s	UK
R A Kipp	RCAF	418/FEF	10.5/0.5/1	10.5/0.5/1	UK
G R I Parker	RAF	219	9/1/1 +6 V1s	9/1/1 +6 V1s	UK
A J Owen	RAF	85	9/1/1	15/1/3 +1 V1s	UK
E R Hedgecoe	RAF	85/FIU/151	9/1/1	9/1/1	UK
R Bannock	RCAF	418/406	9/-/4 +18.5 V1s	9/-/4 +18.5 V1s	UK
J O Mathews	RAF	157	9/-/4 +5 V1s	9/-/6 +5 V1s	UK
H E White	RAF	141/BSDU	9/-/2	12/-/4	UK
J R D Braham	RAF	HQ 2 Gp	9/-/-	29/-/5	UK
N E Bunting	RAF	85/488	8/1/2	9/1/2	UK
J G Benson	RAF	157	8/-/3 +6 V1s	10/-/4 +6 V1s	UK
P F L Hall	RNZAF	488	8/1/-	8/1/-	UK
G E Jameson	RNZAF	488	8/-/1	11/-/2	UK
W H Miller	RAF	169/264	8/-/-	11/-/-	UK
G H Goodman	RAF	151	8/-/-	9/-/-	UK
J A S Hall	RAF	85/488	8/-/-	8/-/-	UK
R D Schulz	RCAF	410	8/-/-	8/-/-	UK
E L Williams	RAF	23/605/FEF	7/1/5	7/1/5 +3 V1s	UK
R E Lelong	RNZAF	605/FEF	7/1/3	7/1/3	UK
D A MacFadyen	RCAF	418/406	7/1/- +5 V1s	7/1/- +5 V1s	UK
D T Tull	RAF	219/FIU	7/1/-	8/1/-	UK
K M Hampshire	RAAF	456	7/1/-	7/1/-	UK
J D Somerville	RCAF	410/409	7/-/1	7/-/1	UK
R G Woodman	RAF	169/85/BSDU/410/96	7/-/1	7/-/1	UK
A A Harrington	USAAF	410	7/-/-	7/-/-	UK
B R O'B Hoare	RAF	23/605	6/1/4	9/3/8	UK
A D Wagner	RAF	605	6/1/3	9/-/5 +2 V1s	UK
B J Thwaites	RAF	85	6/1/2	6/1/2	UK
J Singleton	RAF	25/605	6/-/2 +1 V1s	7/-/3 +1 V1s	UK
D Welfare	RAF	239	6/-/2	7.5/1/3	UK
C E Edinger	RCAF	410	6/-/1	6/-/1	UK
D R Howard	RAF	239/BSDU	6/-/-	6/-/-	UK
W H Maguire	RAF	85/FIU	6/-/-	6/-/-	UK
J T Caine	RCAF	418	4+2sh/-/-	4+2sh/-/-	UK
W F Gibb	RAF	264/515/239	5.5/-/-	5.5/-/-	UK
N J Starr	RAF	23/605	5/1/2	5/1/2	UK
C M Ramsey	RAF	264	5/1/-	7/2/-	UK
F E Luma	USAAF	418	5/-/2	5/-/2	UK
W Provan	RAF	29	5/-/2	5/-/2	UK

Name	Service	Sqn/s	Mosquito Claims	Total	Theatre/s
H C Kelsey	RAF	141/169/515/BSDU/BSTU	5/-/1	9/1/2	UK
F J A Chase	RAF	264	5/-/1	5/-/1	UK
R C Pargeter	RAF	29	5/-/1	5/-/1	UK
R T Goucher	RAF	85/151/25	5/-/- +2 V1s	5/-/- +2 V1s	UK
N E Reeves	RAF	239/BSDU/169	5/-/-	14/-/2	UK
M J Gloster	RAF	219	5/-/-	11/-/-	UK
R J Foster	RAF	604	5/-/-	9/1/1	UK
P W Rabone	RAF	23/515	5/-/-	9/-/1	ME/UK
W R Breithaupt	RCAF	409/239	5/-/-	5/-/-	UK
R I E Britten	RCAF	409/604	5/-/-	5/-/-	UK
D L Hughes	RAF	239	5/-/-	5/-/-	UK
K W Stewart	RAF	488	5/-/1	5/-/1	UK
H B Thomas	RAF	85	5/-/-	5/-/-	UK
J R F Johnson	RCAF	418	2+3sh/0.5/1	2+3sh/0.5/1	UK
H D Cleveland	RCAF	418	4.5/-/-	4.5/-/-	UK
C L Jasper*	RCAF	418	4/-/- +3 V1s	4/-/- +3 V1s	UK
A E Browne*	RNZAF	488/89	4/-/-	4/-/-	UK/FE
W G Kirkwood*	RCAF	409/406	4/-/-	4/-/-	UK
D N Robinson*	RAF	488	4/-/-	4/-/-	UK
R Park*	RAF	256	3/-/1	3/-/1	ME

Note: Those pilots with less than 5 victories are marked thus * and are shown because of their inclusion in Christopher Shores' *Aces High*, and where there may be doubt as to their actual scores

Theatre Abbreviations
UK - United Kingdom and North-West Europe
ME - North Africa/Mediterranean and Italy
FE - Far East and Australia

Aces With Some Mosquito Claims

Name	Service	Sqn/s	Mosquito Victories	Total	Theatre/s
E D Crew	RAF	85/96	4/-/2 +21 V1s	12.5/-/5 +21 V1s	UK
J Cunningham	RAF	85	4/1/1	20/3/7	UK
G L Howitt	RAF	85/456/125	4/1/- +2 V1s	6/1/1 +2 V1s	UK
D H Greaves	RAF	25	4/1/-	9/1/1	UK
J G Topham	RAF	125	4/-/1	13/1/1	UK
I H Cosby	RAF	264	4/-/1 +2 V1s	5.5/1/2 +2 V1s	UK
M M Davison	RAF	264	4/-/- +1 V1	12/1/1 +1 V1s	UK
R B Cowper	RAAF	456	4/-/- +1 V1	6/-/1 +1 V1s	UK
L Stephenson	RAF	219	4/-/-	10/-/-	UK
P G K Williamson	RAF	219/23	4/-/-	9/-/-	UK
D H Blomely	RAF	605	4/-/-	5/-/-	UK
J C Surman	RAF	604	4/-/-	5/-/-	UK
D J Williams	RCAF	410/406	3.5/-/-	5.5/-/-	UK
M H Constable-Maxwell	RAF	264/604/84	3/2/1	6.5/4/2	UK/FE
R A Miller	RAF	604/FIU	3/1/1	7/1/2	UK
A J Hodgkinson	RAF	264/23	3/-/1	12/1/5	UK
P L Burke	RAF	264/219	3/-/0.5 +2 V1s	5/1/0.5 +2 V1s	UK
C M Wight-Boycott	RAF	25	3/-/- +2 V1s	7/-/2 +2 V1s	UK

Name	Service/Nationality	Sqn/s	Mosquito Victories	Total	Theatre/s
S Heglund	Norwegian	85	3/-/-	14.5/5/6.5	UK
J A M Haddon*	RAF	604/264	3/-/-	4/-/-	UK
P G Wykeham-Barnes	RAF	23/140 Wg	2/-/1	14+3/1/2+2sh	ME/UK
I S Smith	RAF	151/487	2/-/1	8/1/4	UK
H E Bodien	RAF	151/21	2/-/1	5/-/1	UK
E G Barwell	RAF	125/264	2/-/- +1 V1	9/11 +1 V1	UK
F D Hughes	RAF	604	2/-/-	18.5/1/1	UK
R A Chisholm	RAF	FIU	2/-/-	9/1/1	UK
H W Eliot	RAF	256	2/-/-	8.5/1.5/1	ME
P S Kendall	RAF	85	2/-/-	8/1/2	UK
C A Cooke	RAF	264/151	2/-/-	5.5/3/1	UK
C M Miller*	RAF	85	2/-/-	4/-/-	UK
R C Haine*	RAF	488	2/-/-	3/-/-	UK
N Russel*	RAF	235	2/-/-	3/-/-	UK
F R L Mellersh	RAF	96/FIU	1/-/- +39 V1s	8/1/- +39 V1s	UK
A E Marshall	RAF	25	1/-/- +1 V1	16+2sh/2/1 +1 V1	UK
R C Fumerton	RCAF	406	1/-/-	14/-/1	UK
G L Raphael	RAF	85/Manston	1/-/- +2 V1s	7/1/1 +2 V1s	UK
R F H Clerke	RAF	1 PRU/157	1/-/-	4+3sh/2+2sh/-	UK
B R Keele	RAF	85	1/-/-	6/-/1	UK
A G Lawrence	RCAF	410	1/-/-	5/-/-	UK
J B Selby	RAF	23	1/-/-	5/-/-	UK
K T A O'Sullivan*	RAF	125	1/-/-	4/-/1	UK
G L Denholm	RAF	605	-/1/-	3+3sh/3.5/6	UK
J H Etherton	RAF	151/176	-/-/2	6/-/3	UK/FE
R A Mitchell	RAF	605	0.5/-/-	5+3sh/3/9	UK
M J Mansfeld	Czech	68	2 V1s	8+2sh/-/2 +2 V1s	UK
K G Rayment	RAF	264	1 V1	6/1/1 +1 V1	UK
H deC A Woodhouse	RAF	51 OTU	1 V1	3+2sh/-/4 +1 V1	UK

V1 Aces With Mosquito Claims

Name	Service	Sqn/s	V1 Victories	Mosquito Victories	Total Victories
R N Chudleigh	RAF	96	15	-	2/-/-
J L T Robb	RAF	85	13	1/-/1	1/-/1
I A Dobie	RAF	96	13	1/-/-	1/-/-
D L Ward	RAF	96	12	2/-/-	3/-/-
J G Musgrave	RAF	605	12	-	-
A Parker-Rees	RAF	96	9	3/1/-	3/1/-
K A Roediger	RAAF	456	9	2/-/-	2/-/-
B F Miller	USAAF	605	9	1/-/2	1/-/2
B G Bensted	RAF	605	8	-	-
J Bryan	RAF	96	8	-	-
G C Wright	RAF	605	8	-	-
W A McLardy	RAF	96	6+2sh	-	-
N S Head	RAF	96	7	4/2/-	4/2/-
J H M Chisholm	RAF	157	7	-	-
C J Evans	RCAF	418	7	1.5/1/-	1.5/1/-
J Goode	RAF	96	6.5	-	-
W J Gough	RAF	96	6	2/1/-	2/1/-

Name	Service	Sqn/s	V1 Victories	Mosquito Victories	Total Victoriess
G L Caldwell	RAF	96	6	1/-/-	1/-/-
R C Walton	RAF	605	6	-	-
P deL Brooke	RAF	264/85	5	3/-/-	3/-/-
B Howard	RAAF	456	5	3/-/-	3/-/-
B Williams	RAF	605	5	1/-/2	1/-/2
P S Leggat	RCAF	418	5	-	-
N S May	RCAF	418	5	-	-
J C Worthington	RNZAF	605	5?	-	-

Aces With No Mosquito Claims

Name	Service/Nationality	Sqn/s	Total	Theatre
The Hon J W M Aitken	RAF	Banff Wg	14.5/1/3	UK
P F Allen	RAF	125/68	5/2/1	UK
K H Blair	RAF	613	6+2sh/5.5/3	UK
A D McN Boyd	RAF	219	10/-/-	UK
A H Boyd	RAAF	67 RAAF	6.5/3/3	FE
D H Cartridge	RAF	254	2+3sh/-/-	UK
P C Cobley*	RAF	613	2/-/6	UK
G B S Coleman	RAF	600	7/1/1	ME
A B Downing	RAF	169	12/-/-	UK
B V Draper	RAF	45	6.5/2/3	UK
G R Edge	RAF	605	19.5/3/7 at least	UK
A H B Friendship	RAF	604	6+2sh/-/1	UK
A Glowaki	Polish	307	8.5/3/5	UK
E J Gracie	RAF	169	7+3sh/5/6	UK
H H K Gunnis	RAF	248	5/2/1	UK
D H Hammond*	RAF	489	1+2sh/1/1	UK
M J Herrick	RNZAF	305	6+2sh/-/2	UK
A W Horne	RAF	605	7/-/-	UK
J H Kilmartin	RAF	AHQ SEA	13+2sh/-/1	FE
J R Kilner	RAF	21	3+2sh/4/2	UK
J V Kucera	Czech	544	5/-/0.5	UK
K M Kuttelwascher	Czech	23	18+2sh/2/5	UK
P B Lucas*	RAF	613	1+2sh/1/8.5	UK
G H Melville-Jackson	RAF	333/618/47	2+3sh/-/-	UK/FE
D S Pain	RAF	219	5/-/-	UK
J H Player*	RAF	249	4/-/-	ME
H P Pleasance	RAF	22	5/1/2	FE
G F Powell-Sheddan	RAF	29	4+2sh/2sh/-	UK
S W Rees	RAF	600	6/-/1	ME
A J Rippon	RAF	107	4+3sh/-/0.5	UK
F N Robertson	RAF	96	11.5/3/7	UK
D W Schmidt	RAF	404	8.5/1/5.5	UK
H Steere	RAF	627	6+5sh/2/-	UK
D A Thompson	RAF	600	5/-/1	UK
E R Thorne	RAF	169	12.5/-/2	UK
G C Unwin	RAF	613	13+2sh/2/1	UK

Colour Plates

1
Mosquito NF II DD673/YP-E of Sqn Ldr N J Starr, No 23 Sqn, Manston, 23 August 1942

'Jackie' Starr was a flight commander with No 23 Sqn, and on one of its first operations he took off from Manston in this aircraft for the Dutch airfield at Deelen. However, some ten miles off the enemy coast the aircraft's port engine failed and so he returned to base. On landing, DD673 collided with a steamroller, although the crew were uninjured. Starr became a successful intruder pilot, achieving five victories before being killed in a flying accident on the way to his wedding in late January 1945.

2
Mosquito FB VI HJ675/YP-V of Flt Lt P W Rabone, No 23 Sqn, Luqa, Malta, 8 July 1943

HJ675 became Paul Rabone's regular aircraft after he joined No 23 Sqn, and he first flew it on an intruder to Sicily on the night of 6 July. On the 20th he was again at the controls when he made a damaging attack on the Italian seaplane base at Lake Bracciano, strafing three Z506Bs at anchor. Rabone also used HJ675 on 8 September when he flew to Grossetto airfield, on the Italian west coast, and sent down a Ju 88 to claim his all-important fifth victory. A few minutes later Rabone attacked and shot down an He 111. This aircraft was eventually lost in a crash on 10 September 1944 whilst serving with No 308 Maintenance Unit.

3
Mosquito NF XXX MT487/ZK-L of Flt Lt D H Greaves, No 25 Sqn, Castle Camps, October 1944

Greaves and his navigator Milton Robbins began flying Mosquitoes with No 25 Sqn in January 1944 and enjoyed several successes during the 'Baby Blitz'. In the autumn of that year the pair regularly flew MT487, with their first patrol in the aircraft taking place on 24 October. It was also occasionally flown by another very successful pilot, Flt Lt Alfred Marshall, before his loss in late November. Shortly before this, Greaves had shot down a V1-launching He 111 for his ninth, and last, victory. MT487 flew No 25 Sqn's final operational sortie of the war with Flt Lt F M Slater at the controls.

4
Mosquito FB VI RF942/KU-H of Wg Cdr G H Melville-Jackson, No 47 Sqn, Kemajoran, Java, November 1945

In the aftermath of the Japanese surrender, several Mosquito units flew operations against Indonesian separatists in Java. One of the detachments involved came from No 47 Sqn, which was led by Coastal Command ace George Melville-Jackson. The squadron began operations late in November, and flying this aircraft on the 29th, Melville-Jackson and his navigator, Flt Lt Wise, covered troops to the east of Batavia, where they spotted a road block and demolished the strongpoint with well-aimed rocket projectiles. The following day he led a combined strike of RAF Mosquitoes and Thunderbolts in the Ambarawa area. RF942 was struck off charge in April 1947.

5
Mosquito NF XII HK119/VY-S of Flg Off B A Burbridge, No 85 Sqn, West Malling, August 1943

Branse Burbridge flew HK119 regularly through the summer and autumn of 1943, having made his first sortie in the fighter on 4 August. Prior to this, on the night of 29/30 May, Flt Lt John Lintott had used HK119 to shoot down the first Ju 88S to fall on English soil, giving him the third of his four victories. Several other No 85 Sqn aces also flew HK119, including Flt Lt E R Hedgecoe (nine victories), Sqn Ldr Bill Maguire (six) and Flt Lt Bernard Thwaites (six). It was subsequently written off in a crash-landing whilst serving with No 307 Sqn on 27 June 1944.

6
Mosquito NF XXX NT484/VY-B of Capt S Heglund, No 85 Sqn, Swannington, March 1945

In late 1944 leading Norwegian ace Svein Heglund managed a return to operations with No 85 Sqn, and he quickly established himself by shooting down three Bf 110 nightfighters over Germany. NT484 was first flown by Heglund and his navigator, Robert Symon, on 17 March 1945 when they sortied on a bomber support mission, landing at Cambrai. They later flew this aircraft on several other operations, and NT484 also took part in No 85 Sqn's final wartime mission.

7
Mosquito NF XXX NT585/VA-H of Wg Cdr G L Howitt, No 125 'Newfoundland' Sqn, Church Fenton, May 1945

By the time he assumed command of No 125 Sqn in December 1944, Geoffrey Howitt was a distinguished nightfighter ace with six confirmed victories. He continued to fly operations until war's end, but did not actually fly NT585 until the day before the German surrender, when he and Flt Lt George Irving (his long-standing navigator) flew some practice intercepts. It then became his regular aircraft until he left the unit in October.

8
Mosquito NF XII HK183/DZ-W of Sqn Ldr H E Bodien, No 151 Sqn, Middle Wallop, August 1943

A pre-war RAF apprentice, Henry Bodien joined No 151 Sqn in 1941, and by mid 1943 he was a flight commander with five victories, including two on the Mosquito, to his credit. In May of that year the squadron had begun to receive the improved NF XII, including HK183, which Bodien and his navigator flew on a number of occasions just prior to his departure from the unit at the completion of his tour in August. This aircraft was written off shortly afterwards, on 24 November 1943, in a landing accident at Colerne.

9
Mosquito NF II DD612/RS-G of Sqn Ldr R F H Clerke, No 157 Sqn, Castle Camps, August 1942

In 1942 Rupert Clerke joined the RAF's first nightfighter unit, No 157 Sqn, as a flight commander, and he became an ace on 30 September. He flew this aircraft on a number of occasions during the late summer of 1942, despite it being the regular mount of his CO, Wg Cdr R G Slade, who engaged a Do 217 over Norwich in it during June. DD612 was also used by Sqn Ldr Glyn Ashfield when he damaged a Ju 88 on 19 October – his fifth overall claim. This aircraft ended its days as an instructional airframe in June 1943.

10
Mosquito NF XIX MM653/RS-L of Sqn Ldr J G Benson, No 157 Sqn, Swannington, 30 October 1944

Sqn Ldr 'Ben' Benson and his navigator Flt Lt Lewis Brandon were No 157 Sqn's most successful crew. They first flew this aircraft on the night of 30 October 1944 on a bomber support intruder to the Cologne area. There, they gained two radar contacts that proved to be friendly – one was a Lancaster and the other a Liberator. Although Benson and Brandon did not claim in this aircraft, MM653 did gain success when, on the night of 17 December 1944, it shot down a Bf 110 whilst being flown by Flt Sgt Leigh.

11
Mosquito NF XXX NT336/FK-P of Flt Lt G R I Parker, No 219 Sqn, B 48 Amiens/Glisy, France, February 1945

'Sailor' Parker had served on loan with the Royal Navy as an observer in Fulmar fighters early in the war, and after pilot training he joined No 219 Sqn in 1944. Parker enjoyed great success with this unit, claiming nine aircraft and six V1s confirmed destroyed. NT336 was delivered to No 219 Sqn at Amiens in early 1945, and it flew its first sortie on 1 February. Parker and his navigator, Wt Off D L Godfrey, flew it for the first time on a defensive patrol one week later. This aircraft served with No 23 Sqn post-war.

12
Mosquito FB VI HR118/3-W of Flg Off N Russell, No 235 Sqn, Portreath, 18 July 1944

Noel Russell was a coastal strike pilot who had enjoyed several successes flying Beaufighters during 1942. He later joined No 235 Sqn and flew Mosquitoes on anti-shipping operations, again with considerable success. After D-Day, the squadron flew patrols over the Bay of Biscay, during which time Russell and his navigator, Flg Off Tom Armstrong, often sortied in HR118. Their first flight in the aircraft occurred on 18 July, when they escorted some Royal Navy frigates. This aircraft crash-landed and was written off at Lossiemouth on 22 February 1945 whilst serving with the Norwegian-manned No 333 Sqn.

13
Mosquito NF XXX NT362/HB-S of Wg Cdr W F Gibb, No 239 Sqn, West Raynham, February-April 1945

Walter Gibb assumed command of No 239 Sqn at West Raynham in September 1944, his unit supporting night bombing raids on Germany. During February and March 1945, with his navigator Flg Off Bob Kendall, he shot down five Luftwaffe nightfighters, including two on 5 March. Their final victim on the 18th was a deadly He 219. They flew this aircraft on a number of occasions, including on the night of 13 April when Gibb and Kendall led 11 of No 239 Sqn's Mosquitoes in support of a raid on Luneberg. NT362 was also regularly flown by ace Sqn Ldr Dennis Hughes, who achieved his fifth victory on 3 April 1945. This Mosquito was later transferred to the Belgian air force in 1948.

14
Mosquito NF XIII MM582/JT-D of Wg Cdr H W Eliot, No 256 Sqn, Foggia, Italy, December 1944

'Chubby' Eliot made his first claims during 1940 and became an ace over Malta the following year. Converting to nightfighters, he gained further successes before taking over No 256 Sqn in October 1944. Eliot made an immediate impact during intruders to Greece, claiming his final victories. He flew this aircraft during the latter part of 1944, including patrols under 'Turnscrew' GCI on 3 and 4 December. Sadly, the youthful Eliot was shot down and killed by flak in March 1945. MM582 was lost when it crashed into the sea off Nice soon after a night take-off on 19 January 1945.

15
Mosquito NF XIII HK480/PS-P of Sqn Ldr I H Cosby, No 264 Sqn, Church Fenton, April 1944

HK480 joined No 264 Sqn in March 1944 and it was soon in action, for on 20 April the Mosquito was used by Flt Lt John Corre to shoot down an He 177 for the first of his four victories. Two days later it was flown for the first time by Ivor Cosby, who, through the summer, was to claim a further four kills to elevate him to ace status. During the spring HK480 was also occasionally flown by five-kill ace Flt Lt Ken Rayment. It was eventually lost over the Normandy beaches on 24 June when crewed by Flg Offs Fox and Prior.

16
Mosquito NF XIII MM571/PS of Flt Lt K G Rayment, No 264 Sqn, B 17 Caen/Carpiquet, France, September 1944

Ken Rayment had become an ace in the Mediterranean, and in the spring of 1944 he joined No 264 Sqn. During the summer he flew anti-V1 patrols over southern England, shooting down a flying bomb near Portsmouth on 10 July for his only Mosquito claim. By September, No 264 Sqn was based near Caen, from where Rayment occasionally flew MM571 with Flg Off Bone – their first such flight was an uneventful patrol between Amiens and Rouen. For some unexplained reason, the fighter wore unit codes but did not carry an individual letter. Subsequently serving with No 604 Sqn, MM571 was struck off charge in January 1947.

17
Mosquito NF XXX NT283/HU-V of Wg Cdr R Bannock, No 406 Sqn RCAF, Manston, January 1945

Canadian Russ Bannock achieved all his victories when flying the Mosquito. On 23 November 1944 he was given command of No 406 Sqn, which was employed on night intruder work. With his navigator, Flg Off Bob Bruce, Bannock adopted NT283 as their regular aircraft. On the night of 5/6 January, over Josum airfield, the crew stalked and shot down an He 111 and damaged a second, unidentified, aircraft. Their next combat in NT283 was on 4 April, when, over Delmenhorst, they shot down an unidentified enemy aircraft and damaged an Fw 190. This aircraft served on for almost a decade post-war with RAF auxiliary units Nos 609 and 616 Sqns, before finally being retired in 1953.

18
Mosquito NF XIII MM466/KP-G of Flg Off R I E Britten, No 409 Sqn RCAF, B 51 Lille/Vendeville, France, 27/28 December 1944

Canadian Flg Off Ralph Britten joined No 409 Sqn in early 1944, but failed to achieve any aerial successes until late November, when he shot down a Ju 88 over the German/Dutch border. Days later he began flying MM466, which had already seen much action with No 488 Sqn. It was a lucky choice, for on the night of 27 December Britten, with Flt Lt Lowndes, shot down a brace of Ju 88G nightfighters. There was then something of a hiatus due to a reduction in Luftwaffe activity, but in late March 1945, again in this aircraft, Britten enjoyed further success when he shot down a Bf 110. Like most war-weary NF XIIs and XIIIs, MM466 was scrapped (in September 1945) soon after the ending of hostilities in Europe.

19
Mosquito NF XIII HK429/RA-N of Flg Off R D Schultz, No 410 Sqn RCAF, Castle Camps, 13 February 1944

Rayne Schultz and his navigator Flg Off Vern Williams gained four victories during late 1943. In December of that same year they were allocated HK429 as their regular aircraft, and they first flew it on the 21st. It was also flown on occasion by another future ace in Lt Archie Harrington USAAF. On the night of 14 February 1944, Schultz and Williams were flying it off the east coast of England when they intercepted and shot down a Ju 188, although their aircraft was in turn hit by return fire and they just managed to put it back down at Bradwell Bay. Subsequently serving with Nos 604 and 409 Sqns, HK429 was also scrapped within months of VE-Day.

20
Mosquito NF XXX MM788/RA-Q of Flt Lt C E Edinger, No 410 Sqn RCAF, B 48 Amiens/Glisy, France, October 1944

An American citizen, 'Pop' Edinger joined No 410 Sqn in June 1944 and made his initial claims over Normandy. In September the squadron moved to France, from where Edinger and his navigator, Flg Off C C Vaessen, first flew this aircraft on the night of 18 October and occasionally thereafter, although they made no claims in it. MM788 was the regular aircraft of Flt Lt Walter Dinsdale, who used it on 27 December to shoot down a Ju 88 over western Germany to score his third, and final, victory. This aircraft was lost in a take-off accident at B 48 on 7 March 1945.

21
Mosquito FB VI NS850/TH-M of Flt Lt R A Kipp, No 418 Sqn RCAF, Holmsley South, 14 April 1944

On 14 April 1944 Robert Kipp and his navigator Flt Lt Peter Huletsky set out with another Mosquito on a Day *Ranger* to Denmark. Over the Kattegatt, Kipp engaged two Ju 52/3ms fitted with minesweeping rings and shot both of them down, so achieving ace status. Coincidentally, his wingman, Flg Off John Caine, also shot down two Junkers minesweepers to become an ace too. Kipp then attacked an airfield, destroying two Do 217s on the ground and damaging a third, before returning home at the end of a very successful sortie. Kipp received a DFC soon afterwards. His aircraft was named *Black Rufe*, and it was wrecked in an landing accident at Hunsdon on 1 November 1944.

22
Mosquito NF XXX NT311/RX-L of Sqn Ldr R B Cowper, No 456 Sqn RAAF, Bradwell Bay, March 1945

Australian Bob Cowper achieved ace status in England as a flight commander with No 456 Sqn soon after D-Day, claiming his final victory on 4/5 July. However, lack of enemy activity meant that the eager Cowper and his navigator, Flt Lt Bill Watson, were left to become increasingly frustrated for the remainder of their tour, flying fruitless defensive patrols. The pair first flew this aircraft on 4 March 1945, when 70+ enemy intruders roamed over East Anglia and Lincolnshire looking for heavy bombers. Cowper and Watson failed to gain any contacts, however.

23
Mosquito FB VI MM417/EG-T of Wg Cdr I S Smith, No 487 Sqn RNZAF, Hunsdon, March 1944

'Blackie' Smith had claimed the first ever Mosquito nightfighter victories in June 1942, and he later returned to operations as CO of No 487 Sqn, leading the unit on the famous Amiens prison raid in FB VI EG-R. He preferred to fly MM417 EG-T, however, and on 26 March, with navigator Flt Lt R A Nash, he led an attack on coastal defence emplacements under construction at Les Hayes. MM417 was hit by flak during the mission and Smith was forced to crash-land at Hunsdon. The FB VI was wrecked, but the crew escaped without injury.

24
Mosquito NF XIII MM466/ME-R of Flt Lt G E Jameson, No 488 Sqn RNZAF, Colerne, 29/30 July 1944

MM466 was the RAF's most successful Mosquito in terms of aerial victories, with eight of its successes coming when flown by 'Jamie' Jameson and his navigator Norman Crookes. The pair scored their first kills with the aircraft on the night of 24 June 1944 when they shot down a Me 410 over the Normandy beachhead. Again in MM466, Jameson became an ace four nights later. A month after that the pair were again over Normandy in this aircraft when, in very poor weather, Jameson and Crookes destroyed no fewer than four enemy bombers in their best return of the war. The following month, having shot down a further two Ju 88s, again in MM466, and taken his total to 11, Jameson was repatriated home. MM466 later served with No 409 Sqn, before being struck off charge in September 1945.

25
Mosquito NF XXX NT370/ME-P of Flt Lt J A S Hall, No 488 Sqn RNZAF, B 48 Amiens/Glisy, 23 March 1945

John Hall claimed all of his victories flying Mosquitoes, becoming an ace shortly before D-Day. In the late evening of 26 March 1945, with navigator Plt Off T F Taylor, he took off in this aircraft to patrol the newly established bridgehead over the Rhine and soon located 'trade' in the shape of a Ju 88. After two well aimed bursts of cannon fire, Hall's final victim fell in flames, but debris badly damaged NT370. Hall managed to fly to Gilze-Rijen, in Holland, where he successfully made a wheels up landing. Although both he and Taylor emerged from the smoking Mosquito unscathed, the aircraft was quickly consumed by flames.

26
Mosquito FB VI RS575/3P-V of Wg Cdr H C Kelsey, No 515 Sqn, Little Snoring, February-April 1945

In late 1944 Howard Kelsey assumed command of No 515 Sqn, and on Christmas Eve he claimed three aircraft destroyed on the ground. In early 1945 he began flying RS575 regularly, scoring his first success in it on 2 February when he shot down a Ju 88. A week later, during an intruder, Kelsey shot down another Junkers bomber and damaged a second, again in RS575. His final success was also in this aircraft when, during the night of 24 April, he claimed No 100 Group's very last Mosquito victory of the war – a Do 217 that he downed near Prague. RS575 remained in RAF service post-war until 1954.

27
Mosquito NF XIII MM465/NG-X of Wg Cdr M H Constable-Maxwell DFC, No 604 'County of Middlesex' Sqn, Colerne, 3 July 1944

MM465 was the personal aircraft of Michael Constable-Maxwell, and in it he claimed his last two victories with his long-time navigator, Flt Lt John Quinton. On the night of 2/3 July, over Normandy, they destroyed a Ju 88, followed by a second Junkers bomber shot down and a Do 217 probable a few nights later. On relinquishing command, Constable-Maxwell passed MM465 on to his successor, and fellow ace, Wg Cdr Desmond Hughes, who immediately used it to good effect by shooting down a Ju 88 at the beginning of August for his penultimate victory. MM465 ended the war serving with No 264 Sqn.

28
Mosquito NF XIII MM552/NG-N of Flt Lt R J Foster, No 604 'County of Middlesex' Sqn, Colerne, 3/4 August 1944

Late on 3 August 1944, Jack 'Fingers' Foster and his navigator, Flg Off 'Ping' Newton, were on patrol over Normandy in this aircraft in fine weather when they attacked a Do 217. Foster later described pulling the nose up and firing a two-second burst into the bomber from 150 yards as the Dornier turned gently to starboard. A second burst resulted in an explosion from the fuselage and port engine, before the Do 217 dived away. They attacked again, scoring further hits just prior to the aircraft crashing south of Granville, giving Foster his fifth victory. It was also his first of five on the Mosquito. Like MM465, this aircraft was also subsequently passed on to No 264 Sqn.

29
Mosquito NF II DZ716/UP-L of Wg Cdr G Denholm, No 605 'County of Warwick' Sqn, Ford, March 1943

A pre-war Auxiliary and Battle of Britain ace, George Denholm joined No 605 Sqn as its CO in 1942, and early the following year he supervised its conversion to Mosquitoes in the intruder role. DZ716 soon became his personal mount, and he used it to fly the squadron's first Mosquito operation on 10 March. The following night Denholm flew to Gilze-Rijen, where he made No 605 Sqn's first Mosquito claim by probably destroying an unidentified aircraft in the area. Denholm left the unit soon afterwards. This Mosquito was written off in a crash-landing at Castle Camps on 7 July 1943.

30
Mosquito FB VI NS838/UP-J of Flt Lt A D Wagner, No 605 'County of Warwick' Sqn, Bradwell Bay, 5 March 1944

Nine-kill ace Alan Wagner and his navigator Flg Off 'Pip' Orringe were flying this aircraft, which bore the name *WAG'S WAR WAGON*, on an intruder over Germany on the night of 5 March 1944 when, near a well-lit airfield at Gardelegen, they shot down an Fw 190. Minutes later the crew also destroyed two Me 410s, one of which blew up and scorched the Mosquito. Wagner then used his remaining ammunition on another Me 410, but it could only be claimed as damaged.

BIBLIOGRAPHY

Banks, Capt R D, *From Whitecaps to Contrails*. CFB Shearwater, 1981
Bennett, Sqn Ldr John, *Fighter Nights*. Banner, 1995
Bowman, Martin & Cushing, Tom, *Confounding the Reich*. PSL, 1996
Braham, Wg Cdr J R D, *Scramble*. Pan, 1963
Chisholm, Roderick, *Cover of Darkness*. Chatto & Windus, 1953
Flintham, Vic & Thomas, Andrew, *Combat Codes*. Airlife, 2003
Griffin, John & Kostenuk, Samuel, *RCAF Squadron Histories & Aircraft*. Samuel Stevens, 1977
Halley, James, *Squadrons of the RAF & Commonwealth*. Air Britain, 1988
Herrington, John, *Australians in the War 1939-45*, Series 3 Volume 3. Halstead Press, 1962
Jefford, Wg Cdr C G, *RAF Squadrons*. Airlife 1988 & 2001
Kitching, T W, *From Dusk Till Dawn*. FPD, 2001
McAulay, Lex, *Six Aces*. Banner, 1991
Milberry, Larry & Halliday, Hugh, *The RCAF at War 1939-1945*. CANAV, 1990
Nesbit, Roy C, *The Strike Wings*. William Kimber, 1984
Onderwater, Hans, *Gentlemen in Blue*. Leo Cooper, 1997
Rawlings, John D R, *Fighter Squadrons of the RAF*. Macdonald, 1969
Rawlings, John D R, *Coastal, Support and Special Squadrons of the RAF*. Jane's, 1982
Rawnsley, C F & Wright, Robert, *Night Fighter*. Corgie, 1966
Richards, Denis, *RAF Official History 1939-45*, Parts 1 & 2. HMSO, 1954
Rudd, Peter, *The Red Eagles*. Peter Rudd, 1995
Shores, Christopher, *Aces High* Vol 2. Grub St, 1999
Shores, Christopher, *Those Other Eagles*. Grub St, 2004
Shores, Christopher & Williams, Clive, *Aces High* Vol 1. Grub St, 1994

INDEX

References to illustrations are shown in **bold**. Plates are shown with page and caption locators in brackets.

Allan, Sqn Ldr J W 'Ian', DFC 16, 78, **79**, 79–80, 81
Armstrong, Flg Off (later Flt Lt) Tom **47**, 93

Bannock, Sqn Ldr (later Wg Cdr) Russ **17**(54, 93), 70, **72**, 72, 75
Bellis, Flg Off (later Flt Lt) D B 'Taff' 66, **68**, 69
Benson, Flt Lt (later Sqn Ldr) J G 'Ben' 13, **10**(52, 93), 69, 72, 73
Bodien, Flt Lt (later Sqn Ldr) Henry E 16, 44, **8**(51, 92)
Bone, Plt Off (later Flg Off) Freddie 66, 69, 93
Braham, Wg Cdr Bob **44**, 44, 45, 46
Brandon, Flt Lt Lewis 13, 69, 72, 73, 93
Britten, Flg Off (later Flt Lt) Ralph I E **37**, 41, **18**(54, 94)
Browne, Sqn Ldr Allan **84**, 85
Bruce, Plt Off (later Flg Off) Robert 'Bob' **10**, **72**, 93
Brumby, Flg Off H E 'Bill', DFC **39**, 40, 42
Bulge, Battle of the 38–39
Bullock, Flt Lt 'Tiny' 72–73
Bunting, Flt Lt (later Sqn Ldr) Nigel 10, 12, 17–18, 28, 31
Burbridge, Flg Off (later Wg Cdr) Branse, DSO* DFC* 22–23, 24–25, 69–70, **71**, 72, 73, **87**, 87
  as Flg Off 9, **14**, **19**, 19, **5**(50, 92)

Caine, Flg Off (later Flt Lt) John 63, 64, 75, 87, 94
Chase, Sqn Ldr John 28–29, 34
Chisholm, Wg Cdr 'Rory' 17, 61–62
Clarke, Flt Lt Frank 61–62
Clerke, Flt Lt (later Wg Cdr) Rupert 6, **9**, 9–10, **9**(51, 92–93), 76
Cleveland, Sqn Ldr Howie **63**, 64, 67–68
Clifton, Flg Off J L **13**
Cobley, Flt Lt Peter **45**
Constable-Maxwell, Wg Cdr Michael H, DFC **29**, 29–30, **30**, **27**(57, 95), 85
Cooke, Sqn Ldr Charles **8**, 8, 67
Cosby, Flt Lt (later Sqn Ldr) Ivor H 27, 32–33, **15**(53, 93)
Cowper, Flt Lt (later Sqn Ldr) R B 'Bob' 27–28, **20**, **22**(56, 94)
Cramp, Lt **67**
Crew, Sqn Ldr (later Wg Cdr) Edward 14–15, 19, **35**, 35
Crookes, Flg Off Norman **31**, 31–32, 94
Cunningham, Wg Cdr John **11**, 11, 16, 21

Davidson, Flg Off H J, DFC 16, 78, 79–80
Davison, Flt Lt Michael 27, 34
Day, Flt Sgt Frank **63**, 68
de Havilland Mosquito 6, 87
  FB VI 13, 18, **43**, 43, **45**, **2**(49, 92), **c.4**(50, 92), **23**(56, 94), **26**(57, 95), **61**, **63**, 74, 80, 85
  'HR' serials **48**, **12**(52, 93), **67**, 72
  'NS' serials **21**(55, 94), **30**(58, 95), 64
  NF 7, **9**, 10, 46, **1**(49, 92), **9**(51, 92–93), **29**(58, 95), **59**, **60**, **68**, 77
  NF XII **12**, **14**, **5**(50, 92), **8**(51, 92), 79
  NF XIII **12**, 20, **22**, **39**, **15**(53, 93), **19**(55, 94)
  'MM' serials **29**, **33**, **37**, **38**, 14, **37**(53, 93), **16**(54, 93), **18**(54, 94), **24**(56, 94), **27**(57–58, 95)
  NF XIX **10**(52, 93), **71**, **83**, **84**
  NF XXX **4**, **37**, **39**, **3**(49, 92), **20**(55, 94)
  'NT' serials **36**, **33**, **39**, **41**, **6**, **7**(50–51, 92), **11**(52, 93), **13**(53, 93), **17**(54, 93), **22**(56, 94), **25**(57, 94–95), **75**, **86**, **87**
Denholm, Wg Cdr George **29**(58, 95), **60**, 60
Dinsdale, Flt Lt Walter D 26, **39**, 94

Edinger, Flt Lt C E 'Pop' 26, **39**, **20**(55, 94)
Eliot, Wg Cdr Hugh W 'Chubby' **14**(53, 93), **81**, 82
Eriksrud, Sub Lt Finn 46, **47**
Ewing, Flg Off Pete **84**, 84

Finlayson, Flg Off Colin **63**, 64, 68
Finlayson, Flg Off Ross **39**
Foce-Wulf Fw 190A 13–15
Foster, Flt Lt Reg Jack 'Fingers' 32, **40**, 40, **28**(58, 95)

Gibb, Flt Lt (later Wg Cdr) Walter F 12, **13**(53, 93), 74
Goodman, Wg Cdr Geoffrey 66, 66–67
Goucher, Flt Lt Richard 'Dickie' **71**, 72–73
Greaves, Flt Lt Douglas H 23, 36, **37**, **3**(49, 92)

Green, Sqn Ldr (later Wg Cdr) Peter 12, 14, 23, **38**, 38, 39, 40–41
Gregory, Sqn Ldr 'Sticks' **44**, 44, 45

Haddon, Flg Off Jack, DFC **29**
Haine, Wg Cdr Dickie **24**, 24, 34
Hall, Flt Lt John A S 22, **41**, 41, **25**(57, 94–95)
Hall, Flt Lt Peter **22**
Harrington, Lt Archie A **4**, 23, 26, 38, 94
Heglund, Capt Svein **6**(50, 92), **70**, 70–71, **87**
Herrick, Sqn Ldr Mike 45–46
Hoare, Wg Cdr B R O 'Bertie/Sammy', DSO **8**, 8, 59, 60, 61, 62
Hodgkinson, Flg Off Arthur 'Hodge' 77, 80
Hooper, Flt Lt John 'Hoops' **33**, 33
Howitt, Flt Lt (later Wg Cdr) Geoffrey L 12–13, 14, **7**(51, 92)
Hubbard, Flg Off S C 'Mum' **33**, 33
Hughes, Wg Cdr Desmond 30, **32**, 33, 40, 95

Jameson, Flg Off (later Flt Lt) G 'Jamie' 29, **31**, 31–32, **24**(56, 94)
Junkers Ju 88 **4**, **24**, 24, **47**

Kelsey, Wg Cdr Howard C **26**(57, 95), **73**, 73, **74**, 75, 86
Kipp, Flt Lt Robert A, DFC **21**(55, 94), 62, 64

Lintott, Flg Off (later Flt Lt) John **14**, 14, 15, 92
Luma, 1Lt James, USAAF **63**, 64

Maggs, Lt **67**
Maguire, Flt Lt (later Sqn Ldr) Bill 16, 19–20, 92
Marshall, Flt Lt Alfred 35–36, **37**, 92
McIlvenny, Flg Off Ralph **29**
McLaren, Flt Sgt (later Plt Off) J A 68, 70
Melville-Jackson, Sqn Ldr (later Wg Cdr) George H **46**, 46, **4**(50, 92), **85**, 85
Messerschmitt Bf 110G-4 **71**
Miller, Plt Off (later Flg Off) W H 'Andy' 66, **69**, 69

Newton, Flg Off (later Flt Lt) Maurice 'Apple/Ping' 32, **40**, 40, 95

operations
  Avalanche 81
  Bodenplatte 40
  Gisela 73–74
  Husky 78
  Neptune 26
  Steinbock 21–24
Orringe, Flg Off 'Pip' 61, **64**, 65, 95

Park, AVM Sir Keith **78**
Parker, Flt Lt G R I 'Sailor' 38, 39, **11**(52, 93)
Phillips, Sqn Ldr (later Wg Cdr) Tony, DSO 47
Pinkerton, Flt Sgt (later Wt Off) 'Pinkie' **84**, 84
Pudsey, Flg Off **10**

Quinton, Flt Lt John 29–30, **30**, 85, 95

Rabone, Flt Lt (later Sqn Ldr) Paul W **2**(49, 92), 69, **80**, 80–81, **81**
Rawnsley, Flt Lt Jimmy **11**, 11, 16, 21
Rayment, Flt Lt Ken G **38**, **16**(54, 93)
Robinson, Flg Off S R 'Jack' 78, **79**
Royal Air Force
  2nd Tactical Air Force 20, 25, 37, 38, 42–43, 86
  Air Defence of Great Britain 20, 26, 35, 66
  Banff Wing 47–48
  Fighter Interception Unit 17, 61–62, 70
  Night Fighter Development Wing 70
  No 1 Photographic Reconnaissance Unit 6
  Nos 10, 11 and 12 Groups 26
  No 85 Group 20, 22, 26
  No 100 Group 62, 64, 65, 69, 72, 73, 75, 86
  No 138 Wing 43
  squadrons
    No 23: **7**, **1**, **2**(49, 92), **59**, 59, 60, 69, 76-78, **77**, **80**, 80, 81
    No 25: 11, 15–16, 22, 35, **37**, **3**(49, 92), 61
    No 27: 83
    No 29: 15, **22**, 22, 25
    No 45: 83–84
    No 47: **4**(50, 92), **85**, 85
    No 68: **36**, 36
    No 85: 10, 11, 12, 13, **14**, 14, 19, **5**, **6**(50, 92), 66, 69, 70, 74, 75, **87**, 87
    No 89: **84**, 85

No 96: 19, 22, 35
No 125 'Newfoundland' 22, 24, **7**(51, 92)
No 141: 62
No 151: 6–7, 16, 22, **8**(51, 92), **67**, **86**, 86
No 157: 6, **9**, 9, **13**, 13, **9**, **10**(51–52, 92–93), 66, 69, **71**, **75**, 75
No 169: 62
No 219: 17–38, 39, 40–41, **11**(52, 93)
No 235: 47, **48**, 48, **12**(52, 93)
No 239: 11, **13**(53, 93), 62, 65, 66, **68**, 75
No 248: 47
No 255: 82–83, **83**
No 256: 15, 16, **14**(53, 93), 78–80, **79**, 81–82
No 264: 7, 8, **10**, 11, 12, 16, 20, 25, 27, 32, 34, 37, **38**, 42, **15**, **16**(53–54, 93), 86
No 307 (Polish) 11
No 333 (Norwegian) **46**, 46
No 515: **26**(57, 95), 62, 69, **74**, 75
No 600: 82, 83
No 604 'County of Middlesex' 20, 25, 29, 30, 32, 33, 37, 40, **27**, **28**(57–58, 95)
No 605 'County of Warwick' **29**, **30**(58, 95), 60, 60–61, 62, **64**, 65, 68, 70
No 613: 43, **45**
Royal Australian Air Force: No 456 Sqn **10**, 11, 22, **22**(56, 94)
Royal Canadian Air Force: squadrons
  No 406: 25, 30, **17**(54, 93), 70, 72
  No 409: 25, **37**, **39**, 42, **18**(54, 94)
  No 410: **4**, 11–12, **12**, 17, 20–21, 22, 25, 26, 37, 38, **39**, **19**, **20**(55, 94)
  No 418: **21**(55, 94), 60, **61**, **63**, 63-65, **72**
Royal New Zealand Air Force: squadrons
  No 487: 43, **23**(56, 94)
  No 488: 19, 20, 22, 24, 25, 38, **39**, **41**, 41, **24**, **25**(56–57, 94–95), 87
Russell, Flg Off (later Flt Lt) Noel **47**, 47, 48, **12**(52, 93)
Russell, Sqn Ldr S P 'Rusty' 76, 81

Scherf, Flt Lt (later Sqn Ldr) Charles, DSO 63, 64–65, 67, 68
Schultz, Sgt (later Flt Lt) Rayne D **12**, 12, 18–19, 20–21, **21**, 42, **19**(55, 94)
Searle, Plt Off L G 78, 79
Selby, Wg Cdr John 78, 80
Shaw, Flt Lt D W **86**
Singleton, Flt Lt Joe 15–16
Skavhaugen, Lt 46
Skelly, Flg Off John 42
Skelton, Flg Off (later Sqn Ldr) Bill, DSO* DFC* 19, 22–23, 25, 69–70, **71**, 73, **87**, 87
Slade, Wg Cdr R Gordon 6, 9, 93
Smith, Sqn Ldr (later Wg Cdr) I S 'Blackie' **6**, 6, 7–8, **43**, 43, **23**(56, 94)
Smith, Sgt Robert 15 Somerville, Sqn Ldr Dean 26, 37
Starr, Sqn Ldr N J 'Jackie' **1**(49, 92), **59**, 76, 77, 78
Stephenson, Flt Lt Leslie 37–38, 39
Stewart, Flt Lt K W 'Chunky', DFC **39**, 40, 42
Surman, Flg Off (later Flt Lt) John 25, **32**, 33–34

Taylor, Plt Off T F 41, 94–95
Thomas, Flg Off (later Flt Lt) Hugh B 20, 74–75
Thomas, Flg Off W F **66**
Thwaites, Flg Off (later Flt Lt) Bernard 14, 18, 19, 92
Tongue, Flg Off D G **4**, 23
Topham, Sqn Ldr (later Wg Cdr) Johnny 22, 28
Turski, Flg Off 45–46

V1 flying bombs 34–37
Vaessen, Flg Off C C 39, 94
Vlotman, Sgt Christiaan 22, **23**

Wagner, Flg Off (later Flt Lt) Alan D, DFC **30**(58, 95), 61, **64**, 65
Watson, Plt Off A F 28–29
Watson, Flg Off (later Flt Lt) Bill 27–28, **28**, 94
Webster, Flg Off Al **39**
Welfare, Flt Lt Dennis 66, **68**, 69
Weston, 'Paddy' 33–34
White, Flg Off Harry 62, 65
Williams, Flg Off (later Wg Cdr) D J 'Blackie' 12, 25, 30–31
Williams, Plt Off (later Flg Off) Leo 61, 76–77
Williams, Flg Off Vern **12**, 12, 18–19, 20–21, **21**, 94
Winn, Sqn Ldr Charles **73**
Wood, Sgt John L 22, **23**
Woodman, Flt Lt Tim 65, 69
Wykeham-Barnes, Wg Cdr Peter 59–60, 76, **77**, **78**, 78
Wyller, Sub Lt 46–47